# THE PASDARAN

## INSIDE IRAN'S ISLAMIC
## REVOLUTIONARY GUARD CORPS

### EMANUELE OTTOLENGHI

## FDD PRESS

A DIVISION OF THE

**FOUNDATION FOR DEFENSE OF DEMOCRACIES**

WASHINGTON, D.C.

For more information about permission to reproduce selections
from this book, write to: research@defenddemocracy.org, or
Permissions, FDD Press, P.O. Box 33249, Washington, D.C. 20033

ISBN: 978-0-9819712-9-2

Cover art: Kamran Jebreili / www.arabianeye.com
Publication design: Basis / www.basisbranding.com

# TABLE OF CONTENTS

# ACKNOWLEDGEMENTS

This work would not have seen the light of day had it not been for the initial vision of my colleagues Cliff May, Mark Dubowitz, and Jonathan Schanzer. My special thanks goes to them and to the Foundation for Defense of Democracies (FDD) for believing in this project and tasking me to complete it. Jonathan and my colleague at FDD, David Donadio, reviewed many earlier drafts of this essay, improving it at each stage both in style and substance. Three distinguished scholars of Iran and great friends—Ali Alfoneh, Reuel Marc Gerecht, and David Menashri—then reviewed it. Each offered unique insights and wise suggestions, thereby enabling me to improve the final product vastly. I wish to thank them all for their invaluable insights and contributions. This monograph would still be a manuscript, gathering dust on my desk, had it not been for the exceptional work of Toby Dershowitz, Annie Fixler, and Jeffrey Maul. They patiently and lovingly took it through all the final steps of proofreading, copy editing, and design, always with enthusiasm and professionalism. My gratitude goes to these three outstanding professionals. Last, but not least, my heartfelt thanks go to my colleague, Laura Grossman, whose invaluable research has ensured accuracy and a wealth of additional information I could not have otherwise found on my own.

Needless to say, while my colleagues all deserve credit for their outstanding input, I am solely responsible for the final outcome of this journey.

The Army of the Guardians of the Islamic Revolution (*Sepah-e Pasdaran-e Enqelab-e Eslami*, or IRGC) is a key force in Iran's internal power structure, as well as in its operations abroad. The IRGC is a conventional fighting force, an economic conglomerate, an agency in charge of nuclear and ballistic missile proliferation, and a player in the country's political system.

Established in 1979 to consolidate the Islamic Revolution and fight its enemies, the IRGC has evolved over the years into a full-fledged conventional army that acts as the regime's Praetorian Guard. It owes its allegiance to the country's highest authority, the Supreme Leader.

The expansion of the IRGC's conventional military capabilities stems in part from the exigencies of national security—first and foremost the Iran-Iraq War (1980-1988), where the IRGC engaged in heavy combat and transformed itself from a revolutionary militia into a professional fighting force. In due course, the IRGC's unswerving loyalty to the regime earned it the control and supervision of Iran's most sensitive defense projects: the ballistic missile and the nuclear programs.

Fighting wars while protecting the regime from internal threats is but one facet of the IRGC's portfolio. As the regime's sword and shield against domestic opposition forces, the Guards engaged in hundreds of assassination operations against dissidents outside Iran's borders and repression inside Iran, including, most recently, after the 2009 presidential elections. But they also constitute a vital instrument of Iranian foreign policy. Among their tasks is the revolution's export abroad, a mission they fulfill through a special branch of the Guards— the Qods Forces—involved in the training, financing, and sponsoring of terrorist groups across the Arab and Islamic world. Through this instrument, Iran has been able to forge alliances, establish client-patron relations, and export deadly fighting methods in the service of its revolutionary goals. Beneficiaries of IRGC training, financing, and support include al-Qaeda and the Taliban, Hezbollah, Hamas and the Palestinian Islamic Jihad, the Sudanese regime, and several Shi'a militias in Iraq.

Since 1989, the Guards have extended their sphere of influence into Iran's economy. Soon after the end of the Iran-Iraq War in 1988, then-president Akbar Hashemi Rafsanjani established the IRGC's Construction Base of the Seal of the Prophets, a.k.a. *Gharargah Sazandegi-ye Khatam-al-Anbiya*, also known as *Khatam-al-Anbiya* or *Ghorb*. *Ghorb*'s specific task is to reconstruct the country and its economy in the spirit of its revolutionary ideals.

*Ghorb* is one of the most powerful enterprises in Iran. It employs approximately 25,000 people, of whom an estimated 10 percent are IRGC conscripts; its many companies are involved in hundreds of projects. Since *Ghorb*'s establishment, the IRGC has built dams, highways, water tunnels, ports, bridges, metro systems, public buildings, pipelines, and other important infrastructure.

Given its origins and history as a reconstruction tool for the Revolution, *Ghorb* initially was involved mainly in infrastructure projects, and it remains heavily invested in that area through its subsidiaries. Most of these projects are straightforward business ventures—although some have military dimensions as well.

Over time, the Guards became involved in other sectors as well—including the food industry, a number of important manufacturing companies, telecommunications, and, more recently, the energy sector where, beyond the initial involvement in the construction of infrastructure projects, IRGC subsidiaries are now directly involved in all phases of the oil supply chain.

IRGC companies are also prominent in the services and logistics sectors, where energy consulting companies, shipping, and harbor logistics (such as bunkering services and containers) also have fallen under the IRGC's purview.

As if all of this were not enough, the IRGC runs additional illicit economic activities through airports and harbors across the country.

The IRGC's involvement in these activities produces vast profits for the organization, which it uses for military procurement and proliferation purposes. The IRGC's legitimate business dealings enable it to gain access to foreign technology that Iran cannot yet produce indigenously. The IRGC can thus acquire missing tools to advance its military projects, learn critical skills, crack technological secrets, and insofar as it succeeds in reverse-engineering foreign technologies, make Iranian military industries less dependent on imports over time.

Given the frequently opaque nature of IRGC involvement in business, it is hard to quantify the combined value of all contracts for which IRGC companies successfully bid. Still, credible estimates suggest the IRGC controls anywhere between 25 and 40 percent of Iran's GDP—the equivalent of tens of billions of dollars. If one considers that the IRGC's share of Iran's GDP in 1989 was around 5 percent, it is remarkable how the organization has expanded as an economic force, both in relative and absolute terms.

The IRGC's expanding economic power eventually heralded its entry into the political sphere, where today its influence is considerable, thanks to the appointment of many of its former senior officers and commanders to influential positions that include provincial governors, members of the Iranian parliament, the Majles, and the cabinet.

The interaction between military, economic, and political power is critical in understanding the IRGC's centrality to Iran's current system; the Guards take advantage of their influence and capabilities in one realm in order to increase their involvement in another. The IRGC's growing economic clout is both an end, in and of itself, and a tool to advance other agendas. Thus, IRGC revenues from economic activities yield political leverage and the resources needed to advance the organization's loyal members in positions of power. The Guards' power, conversely, serves the economic enterprises they own. But the profits inevitably fund their military activities and their involvement in the procurement and development of the nuclear and ballistic missile programs—which in turn enhance their prestige and power within the system. Meanwhile, the Guards' growing political and economic influence enables them to bank on the willingness of public companies to lend their services—both at home and abroad—to aid in the Guards' efforts to procure forbidden technologies and raw materials and to finance their purchases through middlemen in foreign markets.

Nevertheless, in building a commercial empire, the IRGC has conflated its founding mission—regime survival—with its own pecuniary appetites.

The profits the IRGC derives from its business interests fund Iran's military, terrorist proxy groups, and other activities inimical to Western interests. As a result, UN sanctions have singled out the IRGC and its affiliated entities for sanctions. Policymakers should continue to target the Guards' business interests with robust sanctions, blacklisting, and isolation.

Western governments have a duty to expose Iranian companies' connections to the IRGC. Even if official government designations do not always follow, exposure can still discourage business ties. It is important then to identify IRGC entities operating outside Iran, since they may serve as conduits for illegal procurement. Many IRGC entities have one or more overseas subsidiaries to pursue lucrative contracts and acquire valuable technologies. Identifying them can encourage companies to exercise more restraint when looking to sell sensitive technologies. When such transactions occur within the same jurisdictions or between friendly countries, export controls are often less stringent. That is why the IRGC sets up front companies abroad—to facilitate the acquisition of otherwise hard-to-get technology.

Exposing these companies' links to the IRGC can go a long way in reducing their effectiveness.

The Army of the Guardians of the Islamic Revolution (*Sepah-e Pasdaran-e Enqelab-e Eslami*) is more commonly known as Iran's Revolutionary Guards Corps (IRGC). In Persian, it is also known simply as the army, *Sepah*, or guards, *Pasdaran*. The IRGC is a key player in Iran's internal power structure as well as in its operations abroad. The Guards owe their allegiance to the country's highest authority, the Supreme Leader, to whom alone they report. Throughout the years, there have been four Chief Commanders of the IRGC: Mostafa Chamran (1980-1981), Mohsen Rezai (1981-1997), Yahia Rahim Safavi (1997-2007), and Mohammad Ali Jafari (2007 to the present).

The wave of international sanctions passed in recent years by the United Nations (UN), two successive U.S. administrations, Congress, the European Union (EU), and other Western allies all targeted IRGC commanders and affiliated companies for their role in Iran's ballistic missile and nuclear programs.[1] More recently, U.S. and EU sanctions have targeted IRGC commanders for human rights' violations.[2]

The Guards have traditionally played a key role in protecting the Revolution internally against domestic opposition while actively seeking to export it abroad. Established in late 1979 as the Revolution's loyal militia through a merger of various revolutionary forces, the Guards were forged in the crucible of the Iran-Iraq war (1980-1988) and emerged from that conflict as a formidable military force. At that time, the IRGC took control of the clandestine military nuclear program and the ballistic missile program, becoming responsible for Iran's most sensitive, most secretive, and best-funded military endeavors of the past three decades. Yet,

---

1    The UN Security Council has passed six resolutions against Iran to date—1696, 1737, 1747, 1803, 1835, and 1929. Of these, four (1737, 1747, 1803, and 1929) contain sanctions targeting proliferating entities, including IRGC entities and individuals.

2    White House Executive Order on Iran's Human Rights' Abusers, September 29, 2010, www.america.gov/st/ texttrans-english/2010/September/20100929190334su0.9839398.html. See also: www.treasury.gov/resource-center/ sanctions/Documents/13553.pdf; for EU sanctions see:
http://eurlex.europa.eu/LexUriServ/LexUriServ.do?uri=OJ:L:2011:100:0051:0057:EN:PDF and
http://eurlex.europa.eu/LexUriServ/LexUriServ.do?uri=OJ:C:2011:116:0001:0001:EN:PDF.

these programs are but one facet of the Guards' sacred duty to advance Iran's revolutionary goals.

The IRGC is not only the regime's sword and shield against domestic opposition forces. It is also a vital instrument of Iranian foreign policy. In Lebanon, the IRGC operates through its proxy, the Lebanese Shi'a terror group Hezbollah, an organization it helped establish.[3] In Iraq, it works through a host of Iran-sponsored Shi'a militias,[4] as well as Iraq's powerful ministries of defense and interior.[5] Elsewhere in the region, IRGC Special Forces and instructors have supplied weapons, training, and financing, and built a web of alliances with pariah governments like Omar al-Bashir's Sudan,[6] terrorist organizations like the Palestinian Islamic Jihad and Hamas in Gaza, and other deadly groups, such as the Taliban in Afghanistan.

The Guards' role, however, is not limited to military and security matters. Soon after the end of the Iran-Iraq War in 1988, the IRGC secured the means and power to participate in reconstruction efforts—a stepping stone to its rising economic influence today. Since then, the IRGC has gradually become one of the biggest economic interests in the country, growing into an enormous conglomerate of hundreds of companies and financial holdings spanning every sector of Iran's economy. From auto manufacturing to port logistics, from public works such as dams, tunnels, jetties, and highways to petrochemical factories and pipelines, the Guards' work increasingly makes the IRGC the key stakeholder in Iran's economy.[7]

This wealth serves three important goals. First, it generates revenue to finance the IRGC's military-oriented activities—including the nuclear program at home and sponsorship of terrorism abroad. Second, it offers the Guards a network of companies, enterprises, banks, offices, holdings, and joint ventures that can execute the regime's procurement efforts in its quest for advanced weaponry and sensitive

---

3    See Anthony H. Cordesman, *Iran's Support of the Hezbollah in Lebanon*, Center for Strategic, and International Studies, July 15, 2006, http://csis.org/files/media/csis/pubs/060715_hezbollah.pdf.

4    U.S. Department of Defense, *Unclassified Report on Military Power in Iran*, April 2010, www.iranwatch. org/government/us-dod-reportmiliarypoweriran-0410.pdf, pp. 8-9. According to the report, "Iran provides Kata'ib Hizbullah, an Iraqi Shi'a terrorist group, and other Iraqi militant groups with weapons and training."

5    See Kenneth Katzman, *Iran-Iraq Relations*, CRS Report for Congress, August 13, 2010, www.fas.org/sgp/crs/ mideast/RS22323.pdf.

6    The growing bilateral ties between Tehran and Khartoum have been thoroughly reported in Western media for a number of years. See for example, "A New Alliance for Terror?" *Newsweek*, February 24, 1992, www.newsweek. com/1992/02/23/a-new-alliance-for-terror.html#; and Amir Taheri, "Sudan: An Expanding Civil War with an Iran Connection," *The New York Times*, April 9, 1997, www.nytimes.com/1997/04/09/opinion/09iht-edamir.t.html.

7    Mehdi Khalaji, "Iran's Revolutionary Guard Corps, Inc.," *Policy Watch 1273*, The Washington Institute for Near East Policy, August 12, 2007, www.washingtoninstitute.org/templateC05.php?CID=2649.

technology. And third, it generates personal affluence, which the Guards can translate into political influence.

The Guards' rising riches go hand in hand with their increasing power in the political system. In recent years, the IRGC gained more visibility inside Iran's power structure, especially since Mahmoud Ahmadinejad's election as Iran's president in 2005. The number of former IRGC officers sitting in the Majles-e Shura-ye Eslami, or Majles,[8] the popularly elected assembly charged with enacting national legislation, is just one part of their success story. Former IRGC officials sit in the cabinet, rule as provincial governors, represent Iran abroad as ambassadors, run government-owned companies overseas, and fill key positions in or around the office of the Supreme Leader—the country's final arbiter and commander-in-chief.

The IRGC's rise to prominence in Iran's internal power structure alongside its role in running Iran's nuclear program and as the main force behind the wave of violent repression following Iran's 2009 presidential elections finally earned it international attention. This study seeks to shed light on the multifarious nature of the IRGC—its origins and history; its role in terrorist activities abroad and support for proxy forces doing Iran's bidding outside Iran; its economic influence inside Iran; and the way the IRGC uses this expanding economic clout to procure sensitive and forbidden technology abroad.

---

8    According to an opposition report, as many as 80 MPs out of 290 in the current Majles are former members of the IRGC. See "IRGC's Dominance Over Iran's Politics and Economy—Part 1," *Iran Focus*, May 11, 2010, www. iranfocus.com/en/index.php?option=com_content&view=article&id=20355:irgcs-dominance-over-irans-politics-and-economy--part-1&catid=32:exclusive-reports&Itemid=32.

# CHAPTER 2: THE ORIGINS OF THE REVOLUTIONARY GUARDS

Every revolutionary dictatorship has its Praetorian Guard—to intimidate its skeptics, indoctrinate its masses, protect its achievements, promote its vision, export its ideology, and, occasionally, murder its opponents. But such forces—originally created to protect the new order from its enemies—can occasionally become the kingmakers. As a study of the IRGC's role since the 2009 elections notes:

> The Roman Emperor Augustus (27 BC–14 AD) created the Praetorian Guard from among the best and most loyal legionnaires to protect himself from the machinations of generals in the provinces. In time, the Praetorians became a power unto themselves, installing and removing emperors at will. The Islamic Republic of Iran (IRI) today is witnessing the coming of age of its own Praetorian Guard. The Islamic Revolutionary Guard Corps (IRGC), tasked by Ayatollah Ruhollah Khomeini to defend the new regime from its foes after the Iranian Revolution of 1979, has outgrown its original role into a vast social-political-economic-security complex.[1]

The IRGC was established in May 1979, shortly after the Islamic Revolution, by the order of the late Ayatollah Seyyed Ruholah Khomeini, the charismatic founding father of the Islamic Republic of Iran. Khomeini's leadership was enshrined in the Iranian constitution when he was made Supreme Leader, a role that fulfills his religious doctrine of the *velayat-e faqih*. The IRGC is sworn to loyalty to the principle of the *velayat-e faqih* (the Guardianship of the Jurisprudent).

This doctrine, which Khomeini elaborated in his writings, stipulates that the *Faqih*, the Jurist, must guide the body politic, ensuring that its actions conform to Islam and God's will. The Jurist is "God's shadow on earth," and as such, his word is final on what

---

1    Roozbeh Shafshekhan & Farzan Sabet, "The Ayatollah's Praetorians: The Islamic Revolutionary Guard Corps and the 2009 Election Crisis," *The Middle East Journal*, Vol. 64, No. 4, Autumn 2010, p. 543.

constitutes the political realization of divine will. Opposing the Jurist's will is equivalent to opposing God. Anyone found opposing the principle of the Guardianship—whether clergy, opposition groups, or dissidents—is the Guards' enemy and target. Through its oath of loyalty, the IRGC thus sees itself—and is viewed by that portion of the Shi'a clergy, which does not challenge Khomeini's interpretation—as the military arm of God's will.

Much like the principle of the Guardianship of the Jurisprudent, the role of the IRGC was integrated into the new institutional order of the Islamic Revolution. According to article 150 of Iran's 1979 Constitution, the IRGC's main role is to "guard the Revolution and its achievements."[2]

The constitutional architecture of the Iranian Revolution, enacted in December 1979, after nearly a year of internal convulsions, established by law much of what revolutionaries had already imposed on the country by force. The core of what later became the IRGC had already existed since early February 1979 and had helped consolidate the Revolution. During his exile, first in Turkey, then in Iraq, and finally for a few months in France, Khomeini had supported the creation of a revolutionary army—modeled after the Algerian National Liberation Front—among exiled anti-Shah groups. Well before the Shah's regime collapsed, the first volunteers of what grew into the IRGC made their way to Lebanon and Syria to undergo military training under the supervision of the Palestinian Liberation Organization (PLO). Eventually, these volunteers established the nucleus of the IRGC before Khomeini's triumphant return to Iran on February 1, 1979. Some had fought against the Shah in pre-existing militias. Some saw combat in the Lebanese Civil War and their battle readiness proved handy.[3] The Guards' early contacts in Lebanon, in time, would prove equally invaluable in establishing a permanent foothold there. Indeed, the Guards' first commander, Mostafa Chamran, helped establish Islamic revolutionary groups in Algeria, Egypt, Syria, and eventually Lebanon, where he helped create and then fought alongside Amal, the Shi'a militia. But it was Khomeini who ordered the IRGC's establishment and defined its purpose:

> The paramilitary Islamic Revolutionary Guards Corps, whose purpose would be 'to protect the revolution from destructive forces and counter-revolutionaries' was created within weeks of Khomeini's return to Iran on his direct instructions. The Guard was responsible to the Revolutionary

---

2    An English translation of Iran's Constitution is available at: www.iranonline.com/iran/iran-info/government/constitution.html.

3    See Steven R. Ward, *Immortal A Military History of Iran and its Armed Forces*. (Washington, DC: Georgetown University Press, 2009), p. 226: "The Guard initially enlisted six thousand men drawn from those who had fought against the shah's regime before 1978 and had received some guerrilla training with Palestinian and Lebanese groups."

EMANUELE OTTOLENGHI

Council and had its own budget... Recruits... were carefully monitored to ensure that young men from 'communist' or 'eclectic' (People's Mojahedin) backgrounds did not infiltrate the corps. From the moment they entered, they were thoroughly schooled in loyalty to Khomeini and his principles.[4]

Initially, the IRGC served as a military arm of the Revolution, first against the remnants of the Shah's regime, then against those among the opposition who did not sign up to Khomeini's vision of clerical government.

As the hated Shah's departure created a vacuum of authority, different factions vied to shape Iran's future. In the violent confusion that followed the collapse of the transitional government that the Shah had appointed—led by the late Prime Minister Shahpour Bakhtiar—Khomeini's revolutionary vision of an Islamic republic guided by a clerical ruler hung in the balance. Khomeini enjoyed overwhelming support across the political spectrum—but not his vision of Islamic governance. With some notable exceptions, most of the Shah's secular opponents did not believe Khomeini would ultimately impose clerical rule over Iran; they saw him as a unifying figure and a charismatic leader.[5] The revolution's many secular supporters did not share Khomeini's ambitions for Iran. In many cases, they were no less armed than his supporters. Having a devoted militia of well-trained fighters would prove critical to ensure that the new political order would reflect Khomeini's aspirations for his country.

With the Shah no longer in the country and his government in disarray, the army was unable or unwilling to defend a regime that effectively no longer existed. Khomeini's return to Iran, two weeks after the Shah had left Iran, plunged the country into more chaos, as he disavowed the transitional government appointed by the Shah. Pitched battles between revolutionaries and regular forces (or among regular forces themselves) raged until, on February 11, 1979, senior officers realized they could not turn the tide. They issued the order to the army to withdraw from the streets and pledged neutrality.[6] This was an important turning point. February 11 is still celebrated in the annals of

---

4    Baqer Moin, *Khomeini: Life of the Ayatollah*. (London: I.B. Tauris, 2009), pp. 211-212.

5    Khomeini, for his part, had carefully avoided courting controversy by offering the impression, throughout the months leading to the Iranian Revolution, that his goals for Islamic governance were modest and tolerant. As Moin notes, "While emphasizing the principles of Islam, Khomeini at this point spoke of a 'progressive Islam' in which even a woman could become president and in which 'Islamic rules of retribution could not be applied unless sufficient preparations had been made to implement Islamic justice in its totality.' He did not discuss the *velayat-e faqih*... and was careful to sidestep in public the issue of an Islamic state." See Baqer Moin, p. 195.

6    See Ward, p. 224: "Issued at midday, the pronouncement reaffirmed the armed forces' duty to defend Iran's independence and territorial integrity but declared neutrality to avert further chaos and bloodshed. The senior commanders then ordered all military units to return to their barracks."

the Islamic Revolution, since it caused the collapse of the transitional government,[7] but order was not restored for some time after. As revolutionaries gained access to military depots and ammunition on the military bases they stormed, they formed local committees (*komitehs*) to dispense revolutionary justice. With justice administered by popular committees and kangaroo courts tasked with summary trials, executions, and policing tasks, force became indispensable to advance political goals. Other opposition forces that did not embrace Khomeini's vision for an Islamic Republic relied on their own well-armed militias—first and foremost the Communist militia Fedayeen-e Khalq, but also the Islamo-Marxist group Mojahedin-e Khalq (MeK) and various people's Islamic militias. A militia that was loyal to Khomeini, that could countenance the military strength of his opponents, and could also defend the revolution and consolidate its regime, was therefore needed. The IRGC—at first lacking a command structure and even uniforms[8]—took on the Islamic Revolution's enemies. In the process, the IRGC developed into a well-oiled machine of internal repression that included policing, intelligence, and both conventional and non-conventional military capabilities.

Killing opponents, settling scores, and wielding military strength to impose their own order, the Guards eventually emerged as the protectors of the newly established Islamic order and the defenders of the Revolution against enemies, real and imagined. Its forces were forged by the zealotry of revolution, the convulsions of fratricidal conflict, and the crucible of war. They sought to defend the Revolution first against those still loyal to the Shah; then against those centrifugal forces who sought to defect from Iran's new Islamic order; and finally against foreign enemies: chiefly Saddam Hussein's Iraq, and the Revolution's ideological banes, the United States and Israel.

To this day, the liquidation of the Revolution's ideological opponents remains a central objective of the IRGC—a task the Guards zealously fulfilled during the early revolutionary terror that followed the proclamation of the Islamic Republic. Once the Islamic Republic was established, it unleashed the Guards in the country's periphery against the ethnic non-Persian minorities, whose autonomous or separatist aspirations it perceived as a threat to the Revolution.

The earliest challenge the new regime faced undoubtedly came from the Kurdish rebellion that broke out soon after the revolution in the western city of Sanandaj.[9] In mid-March

---

7   The last Shah-appointed prime minister, Shahpour Bakhtiar, went into hiding on February 12, 1979. See Ward, p.224.

8   *Ibid.*, p. 226.

9   For an account of the Kurdish rebellion in the spring of 1979, as well as other clashes involving Iran's ethnic minorities, see Ward, pp. 230-234.

EMANUELE OTTOLENGHI

1979, protesters managed to overcome security forces and take over a police station and army barracks. The rebellion soon spread to other Kurdish towns. As regular forces and the IRGC took turns fighting Kurdish militias, government forces eventually retook control of the cities. For months, however, Kurdish forces kept control of the countryside and the main roads, laying successful ambushes and fighting at night to deny regular forces the advantage of airpower. The Guards' ardor and zeal proved insufficient to surmount the Kurdish rebellion. Their lack of fighting experience and poor coordination with the regular army left them entangled in the treacherous terrain of northwestern Iran well past late September 1980, after Iraq launched its surprise invasion of Iran in the south. As casualties mounted, government forces experienced defeat and desertion, but the Guards refused to tolerate any attempt at a negotiated solution with Kurdish rebels, including the more conciliatory positions of the transitional government. The Guards were determined to crush their enemies, whom they considered unbelievers. Eventually, they subjected the rebellion to brutal force, killing some 5,000 Kurdish fighters and as many as 1,200 civilians for sedition and treason.

If the IRGC's initial inadequacy in responding to the Kurdish rebellion compelled increasing militarization, so too did the Iraqi invasion, which caught the country unprepared. The new regime had purged the military of senior officers and experienced personnel. The army was also undersupplied due to the military embargo the United States imposed after the 1979 seizure of its embassy in Tehran and the resulting hostage crisis. But the Guards threw themselves into the fight, and what they lacked in military expertise and equipment, they initially made up in commitment. Their embrace of martyrdom enabled them to block Iraq's initial thrusts through Iran's ethnically Arab south and quickly gained them the reputation of saviors of the fatherland.

As the war progressed, their role as a politically reliable alternative to the regular army guaranteed them better resources and equipment, which in turn made careers in the IRGC more attractive to young men otherwise destined for the front. The ideological passion and the morbid lure of martyrdom, along with the offer of better pay, more prestige and better opportunities upon finishing one's services enabled the Guards to lure top recruits—even as the war dragged on, and Iran sent its youngest to certain death in wave after wave of pointless military offensives. In time, the IRGC and its veterans emerged from the Iran-Iraq War as the most fearsome defenders of Iran's soil and as the embodiments of Iran's new way of Islamic combat, defined by the triumph of collective martyrdom over a more powerful enemy. Whatever the mythology, the Guards played an important role in the war.

The war, in turn, shaped the Guards and made an army of them. But their trajectory from popular revolutionary militia to a professional fighting force did not take away from the

IRGC's original core objective. Throughout the war years, the IRGC continued to fulfill its task as defender of the Revolution by liquidating the Revolution's enemies. As the war raged in the west, the IRGC turned against its most considerable rival, the MeK, after that group's repeated attacks nearly wiped out the senior echelons of Khomeini's revolutionary leadership.

On June 28, 1981, a powerful bomb went off inside the headquarters of the ruling Islamic Republican Party as a meeting of party leaders was under way. The explosion ripped the building apart, killing 73 party officials, including then chief of the judiciary, Ayatollah Seyyed Mohammad Beheshti, and wounding many others. Though the MeK never claimed responsibility for the attack, it was widely assumed to have planned it. Only a day earlier, another bomb concealed in a tape recorder had severely injured Ayatollah Khomeini's close adviser and confidant, the future president, and current Supreme Leader Ali Khamenei, and permanently cost him the use of his right arm. Then, on August 30, the MeK struck again, this time killing Iran's president, Mohammad-Ali Rajai, and his prime minister, Mohammad Javad Bahonar.

The death and injury of dozens of senior Islamic Republican Party figures gave the regime the pretext it needed to unleash the IRGC on the remaining opposition groups and forced the already embattled MeK leaders to flee abroad, where the Guards eventually hunted them down in the years to come. It was a ruthless, brutal, and gruesome campaign, but it proved as effective as the Bolsheviks' liquidation of their opponents in revolutionary Russia.

The MeK was effectively wiped out of Iran. Those who escaped the IRGC's ferocious reprisals gathered on the Iraqi side of the border, where they sided with their country's arch-enemy, Saddam Hussein. The decision to flee and seek protection under Saddam Hussein's wing may have spared the MeK from the fate of the Communist Tudeh Party (whose liquidation was not completed until the mid-1980s) and the monarchists, whom the Islamic Revolution annihilated as organized political movements. But siding with Saddam Hussein in a war that sent Iranian nationalism aloft left the MeK on the wrong side of history. Though it remains active to this day, and enjoys some backing abroad, the MeK no longer has significant residual popular support in Iran.

The Guards came to fulfill several important functions. Early on, they were entrusted—like political commissars in the Red Army—to ensure that the regular army would not stage a counterrevolutionary comeback. Eventually, the existence of two armies—the regular forces (*Artesh*) and the revolutionary ones (*Pasdaran*)— became a permanent fixture of Iran's military establishment and a reflection of the revolutionary-clerical dualism that permeates all of Iran's state institutions. To most

Iranians, the *Artesh* remained for a long time too compromised by its past loyalty to the Shah to be trusted with defending the homeland in the name of the Islamic Revolution. The IRGC aimed to counterbalance the regular army by both competing with it and keeping it in check.

The exigencies of war meant that the original tasks of the Guards—broadly defined as guarding the Revolution and its achievements—would go well beyond fighting the enemies of the Revolution, fending off counterrevolutionary forces, and exporting Khomeini's vision abroad. The Guards quickly developed into a full-fledged army, with ground troops, a navy and an air force—and eventually a Ministry of the IRGC.[10] The IRGC played key roles in the early stages of the war, before 1982, when Iran sought to absorb and repel Iraq's advances into Iranian territory; in the war's reversal, when, after Iran recaptured its lost territories from Iraq, Khomeini decided it was Iran's turn to invade its neighbor; and in the military offensives that Iran launched inside Iraqi territory after 1982.[11] But the IRGC's ideologically driven blunders in the later phases of the war brought about a direct military confrontation with the United States in 1988, which precipitated Iran's defeat. In a series of reckless acts, the Guards expanded the conflict into the Persian Gulf, threatening merchant shipping by mining ports. The IRGC navy units laid mines at the mouth of the Strait of Hormuz and at the entrance of commercial ports across the region. In response, the U.S. Navy took to escorting ships to protect them from harm. Unhinged by the disparity of forces, the Guards sought direct confrontation with U.S. forces. Their actions eventually led to full-blown conflict after a U.S. ship hit a mine on April 14, 1988. Four days later, the U.S. launched Operation Praying Mantis, which cost Iran dearly. Amid the growing tensions, on July 3, a U.S. Navy ship, the U.S.S. Vincennes, downed an Iranian commercial airliner it mistook for an Iranian fighter jet, killing all 290 passengers on board. Though the downing of the Iran Air Flight 655 was an accident, Iran's leadership believed it was intentional and interpreted the incident as evidence that the U.S. was prepared to do anything to defeat the Islamic Republic. These events eventually forced Iran to agree to a ceasefire and negotiate an armistice treaty with Iraq soon after.

---

10   Eventually, as part of the post-war rationalization of Iran's defense sector, the IRGC ministry was merged with the Ministry of Defense. See Stephen R. Ward, p. 305: "In a victory of more pragmatic leaders over the hard-liners, the Revolutionary Guards Ministry and its subordinate defense procurement and production organizations were merged into the Ministry of Defense to create the Ministry of Defense and Armed Forces Logistics."

11   Discussing the circumstances around the decision, after the battle of Khorramshahr in May 1982 had ended with the IRGC retaking the city, Ali Alfoneh notes that, "Thanks to the war the IRGC had managed to expand its force from a few thousand undisciplined revolutionaries to the most important security, military and even political force in the Islamic Republic. This development would not have been possible had it not been for the continuity of the war with Iraq. In this case it was the IRGC which sacrificed Iran's national interest and hundreds of thousands of Iranian lives for the sake of its expansionist organizational interests." See Ali Alfoneh, "The War over the War," *BBC Persian*, September 30, 2010, www.aei.org/article/102603.

Regardless of its setbacks and shortcomings, the IRGC that emerged from the Iran-Iraq war was a formidable force, with significant political backing, popularity, and access to significant resources to continue to fulfill its tasks. Over time, the IRGC has grown from a ragtag band of revolutionaries tasked with political murder, crowd control, and internal repression to a structured, professional army. Despite its relatively small size, currently estimated at around 130,000 ground forces, 20,000 naval personnel, and 5,000 air force personnel,[12] the IRGC remains a fundamental instrument of Iran's national defense. But the Guards also maintain a special branch dedicated to operations abroad—the Qods Forces (IRGC-QF), which are currently commanded by Major General Qasem Soleimani and have been involved in many operations outside Iran's borders. According to an April 2010 U.S. Department of Defense unclassified report on Iran's military power:

> The Iranian regime uses the Islamic Revolutionary Guard Corps-Qods Force (IRGC-QF) to clandestinely exert military, political, and economic power to advance Iranian national interests abroad. IRGC-QF global activities include: gathering tactical intelligence; conducting covert diplomacy; providing training, arms and financial support to surrogate groups and terrorist organizations; and facilitating some of Iran's provision of humanitarian and economic support to Islamic causes.[13]

According to analyst Anthony Cordesman, in spite of having no more than 15,000 men, the IRGC-QF:

- Enjoys a sizable but classified budget, under direct control of the Supreme Leader.
- Operates abroad through Iranian embassies, enjoying the cover of diplomatic immunity but operating separately, distinctly, and independently of the embassy personnel, which has no access to and no knowledge of its activities.
- Is divided in branches ("corps") assigned to specific regions: Iraq, Lebanon, Palestine, and Jordan; Afghanistan, Pakistan, and India; Turkey and the Arabian Peninsula; Asian countries of the former Soviet Union; North Africa; and Western nations.
- Runs terrorist training camps and related facilities in Lebanon, Sudan, and inside Iran.

---

12   U.S. Department of Defense, *Unclassified Report on Military Power in Iran*, April 2010, www.iranwatch.org/government/us-dod-reportmiliarypoweriran-0410.pdf) pp. 4-6.

13   *Ibid.*,p. 2.

EMANUELE OTTOLENGHI

- Benefits from highly advanced training in unconventional warfare and indoctrination that it uses both to raise its cadres and to train foreign fighters who are ready to fight and die for Iran's revolutionary causes.[14]

Through its overseas operations, the IRGC has struck Iran's enemies near and far, assassinating dissidents in Europe, training Hezbollah in Lebanon, and executing terrorist attacks in France and Argentina.

Finally, to this day the IRGC remains responsible for the indoctrination of the Iranian masses, through a special directorate tasked with propagating the message of the Revolution and keeping its flame alight.

---

14  Anthony H. Cordesman, *Iran's Revolutionary Guards, the Al-Quds Force, and other Intelligence and Paramilitary Forces*, CSIS, August 16, 2007, http://csis.org/files/media/csis/pubs/070816_cordesman_report.pdf, pp. 8-9.

# CHAPTER 3: TERROR IN THE NAME OF THE REVOLUTION: THE IDEOLOGICAL LANDSCAPE OF THE IRGC

A critical component of any revolution is the aspiration to become the radical agent of social and political change. Rarely in history have revolutions stuck to the modest aims of changing the system at home without an eye to exporting the newly established order abroad. Bearing in mind the limits of analogies and precedents in history, Iran's Islamic Revolution featured elements common to many previous revolutionary experiences:

- Iran's Islamic revolutionaries aspired to enact radical change because they saw society as so incorrigibly corrupt that it had to be destroyed and rebuilt from scratch.
- The revolutionaries' religious aspirations transcended the narrow confines of Iranian society and impelled them to pursue ideologically motivated reforms that did not stop at their borders.
- Their desire to export their ideology produced conflict with regional and world powers that did not welcome their revolution.

Revolutionary powers cannot be easily dissuaded through economic incentives. Their projects can be delayed, and they can be denied the means to export their revolution beyond their borders, but revolutionary fervor cannot be quelled by economic inducements. Ideological struggles do not easily lend themselves to appeasement or compromise. Thus, the undiluted pursuit of revolutionary goals will sooner or later put revolutionary powers on a collision course with their neighbors or other powers that see themselves as beneficiaries or guarantors of the *status quo*. Of course, there are few historical circumstances where either the needs of the state or the patient tiring of time did not temper revolutionary fervor. Iran is no exception—and its policies, both domestic and foreign, offer examples where the needs of state, sometimes amplified by the calls of Persian nationalism, have not always prioritized Islam in statecraft. As David Menashri notes:

Once in power, Khomeini—and even more so, his disciples after him—knew they could not rule by means of revolutionary slogans. They were now called upon to manage rather than theorize about affairs of the state. While still allowing allegiance to their revolutionary creed, therefore, a measure of realism was inevitable—not from a newfound moderation, but from a pragmatism responsive to the exigencies of the situation.[1]

Still, pragmatism, when found in restraint, or in choices that put Iran's national interest before Islam, was born out of necessity. It was rarely the first, or favored choice. As Khomeini remarked, in a Persian New Year message delivered on March 21, 1980:

> We must strive to export our revolution throughout the world, and must abandon all idea of not doing so, for not only does Islam refuse to recognize any difference between Muslim countries, it is the champion of all oppressed people... Know well that the world today belongs to the oppressed, and sooner or later they will triumph. They will inherit the earth and build the government of God.[2]

While Khomeini's successors may have occasionally strayed from heeding the call of the Islamic Republic's founder, to this very day, this aspiration remains at the core of the IRGC's mission. Over the years, the IRGC has assiduously pursued this task through a range of activities. It has sought to spur similar revolutionary movements among Shi'a communities abroad. It established and buttressed its Hezbollah franchise in Lebanon, across the Persian Gulf and in Turkey.[3] It has sponsored terrorist acts abroad through proxies and has on several occasions directly engaged in them. The Guards have dispatched assassins abroad to eliminate dissidents and opponents.[4] They have served as bridgeheads in the forging of anti-Western alliances with non-aligned countries, such as Venezuela, beyond the realm of Islam.[5] And they have waged low-intensity war on their mortal ideological enemies—Israel and the United States—causing many casualties and even wreaking havoc on Iran's own national interests.

---

1  David Menashri, "Iran's Revolutionary Politics: Islam and National Identity," in Leonard Binder (Ed.), *Ethnic Conflict and International Politics in the Middle East.* (Gainesville, FL: The University Press of Florida, 1999), p. 132.

2  Hamid Algar, *Islam and Revolution Writings and Declarations of Imam Khomeini (1941-1980).* (North Haledon, NJ: Mizan Press, 1981), pp. 286-287.

3  On February 1, 2011, the U.S. Department of Treasury designated a network of Iranian and Turkish nationals and their companies for procuring sanctioned materials to Iran's Armed Forces industries, AIO: www.treasury.gov/press-center/press-releases/Pages/tg1044.aspx.

4  A list of murdered Iranian dissidents from various political and ethnic backgrounds can be found here: www.iran-e-azad.org/english/terrorlist.html.

5  U.S. Department of Defense, *Unclassified Report on Military Power in Iran*, April 2010, www.iranwatch.org/government/us-dod-reportmiliarypoweriran-0410.pdf, p. 7.

Within months of the Revolution, on November 4, 1979, Iranian revolutionaries seized the U.S. Embassy in Tehran, holding 52 U.S. diplomats hostage for more than a year.[6] The Guards, then in their infancy, played a key role in the crisis.

More important, even as Iran was bogged down in a bloody war against Iraq, the Guards were tasked with establishing a foothold for Iran in Lebanon by organizing the Shi'a community and creating an Islamist counterpoint to the country's other armed factions. As early as 1979, Iranian emissaries started making their way back to Lebanon—a place Iranian revolutionaries had come to know in their days in exile during the 1970s.

Under the guidance of a newly created office tasked to export the Revolution—the Bureau of Assistance to the Islamic Liberation Movements in the World—run by the late Mehdi Hashemi, brother of Grand Ayatollah Hossein-Ali Montazeri's son-in-law,[7] Iran sought to co-opt the Lebanese Shi'a party, Amal, to its cause. Despite Iran's role in establishing Amal, this effort was not successful at first. Amal refused to embrace the doctrine of the Guardianship of the Jurisprudent. By early 1982, Iran decided to create its own organization, and tasked the Iranian ambassador to Damascus, Ali Akbar Mohtashemi-Pour, with coordinating the effort. Eventually, Mohtashemi-Pour managed to gather all the Shi'a factions outside Amal and bring them together under a new umbrella. By the summer of 1982, as Israel entered into a war with Lebanon, Hezbollah was born, and 1,500 IRGC instructors began training its fighters in Baalbek.[8]

Hezbollah, a militia-cum-social and political movement, quickly rose to fame and infamy. Richard Armitage, the former U.S. deputy secretary of state, dubbed the group "the A-team of terrorism" in the Middle East.[9] Though the group is Lebanese, it is a wholly owned IRGC franchise, it subscribes to the principle of *velayat-e faqih*, and it therefore owes its loyalty to Iran's Supreme Leader. With never more than a modest presence of several hundred advisers, the IRGC left an enduring legacy in Lebanon through indoctrination, training, and the introduction of new military tactics previously unknown to the region. The most innovative of these was human bombs, men trained to use explosives—first in a truck or a car, then later, strapped onto themselves—to carry out suicide terror attacks. The notion of human sacrifice as an act of defiance is central to the narrative of

6    The original number was higher but early on in the crisis their captors released a number of female and African-American hostages. For an account of the hostage crisis, see Mark Bowden, *Guests of the Ayatollah*. (NY: Grove Press, 2006).

7    Until early 1989, Montazeri was Khomeini's heir apparent.

8    Shimon Shapira, "The Fantasy of Hezbollah Moderation," *Jerusalem Issue Brief*, Vol. 10, No. 2, May 23, 2010, www.jcpa.org/JCPA/Templates/ShowPage.asp?DBID=1&LNGID=1&TMID=111&FID=283&PID=0&IID=3983.

9    Richard Armitage, *America's Challenges in a Changed World*, remarks at the United States Institute of Peace, September 5, 2002, http://web.archive.org/web/20020917202341/www.state.gov/s/d/rm/2002/13308pf.htm.

Shi'a Islam, through the figure of Hussein ibn Ali, grandson of the Prophet. Hussein's epic and tragic death on the plains of Karbala in 680 CE at the hands of an army sent by the Umayyad Caliph Yazid was not only the trigger for the schism between Sunni and Shi'a Islam. It is also the most defining event of Shi'a tradition and is central to the ideology of martyrdom that in many ways defines the Islamic Republic.

In classical iconography, Hussein is often depicted alone, holding his dying infant son, pleading with Yazid's soldiers. He and his accompanying party of approximately 70 were slain by a much superior force of thousands, and his body was horribly mutilated after his death. Though he surely knew he stood no chance, Hussein nevertheless accepted death as the verdict of heaven, rather than offering his allegiance to Yazid and a political order he considered unjust. There is in his sacrifice a tragic submission to one's destiny—no matter how cruel. There is defiance against evil, though evil will prevail. And there is a surrender of one's own survival instincts to a greater cause. Every generation of Shi'a Muslims has internalized the story of Hussein through poetry, theater, and rituals. Ali Shariati, whose work was in many ways a precursor of the Islamic Republic's ideology, offered a theoretical framework for martyrdom in his writings, which politicized the notion of martyrdom as an instrument to fight oppression. Mixing French philosopher's Frantz Fanon's "cult of purgative and curative violence... with Shiism's cult of worshiping Imam Hussein as the quintessential martyr"[10] Shariati explained:

> A Shahid is the one who negates his whole existence for the sacred ideal in which we all believe. It is natural then that all the sacredness of that ideal and goal transports itself to his existence... Husayn... does not go [into battle with the intention of] succeeding in killing the enemy and winning victory. Neither is he accidentally killed by a terroristic act of someone such as Wahshi. This is not the case. Husayn, while he could stay at home and continue to live, rebels and consciously welcomes death. Precisely at this moment, he chooses self-negation. He takes this dangerous route, placing himself in the battlefield, in front of the contemplators of the world and in front of time, so that [the consequence of] his act might be widely spread and the cause for which he gives his life might be realized sooner. Husayn chose shahadat as an end or as a means for the affirmation of what is being negated and mutilated by the political apparatus.[11]

---

10   Abbas Milani, *Eminent Persians*. Vol. 1, (Syracuse, NY: Syracuse University Press, 2008), p. 365.

11   Ali Shariati, "Jihad and Shahadat. A Discussion of Shahid," www.shariati.com/english/jihadand.html.Cf. Ali Shariati, "Red Shi'ism: The Religion of Martyrdom, Black Shi'ism: the Religion of Mourning," www.shariati.com/english/redblack.html: "bears witness to those who are martyred by the oppression in history, heir of all the leaders of freedom and equality and seekers of justice from Adam to himself, forever, the messenger of martyrdom, the manifestation of the blood revolution."

EMANUELE OTTOLENGHI

Similarly, Iran's clerical revolutionaries cleverly exploited and manipulated this culture of martyrdom, first by attacking the Shah as the cruel ruler of a hereditary monarchy, the same unjust political order which had slain Hussein. Because hereditary monarchy was the dominant system of government among the Gulf Arabs, the original Shi'a grievance against Yazid similarly gave rise to a challenge to the rulers of the region, for whom Khomeini's message meant trouble. Khomeini outlined the reasons why monarchy was incompatible with Islam in a speech delivered in Najaf, during his exile in Iraq, on October 31, 1971:

> The greatest disaster that befell Islam was the usurpation of rule by Mu'awiya from Ali (upon whom be peace), which caused the system of rule to lose its Islamic character entirely and to be replaced by a monarchical regime. This disaster was even worse than the tragedy of Karbala and the misfortunes that befell the Lord of the Martyrs (upon whom be peace) and indeed it led to the tragedy of Karbala.[12]

The indictment of rulers across the Islamic world did not stop at Iran's border. Neither did the call to martyrdom. When Saddam Hussein invaded Iran in 1980, he too became Yazid, and the tens of thousands of young Iranians who rushed to their deaths in the grisly war that followed saw themselves walking in Hussein's footsteps.

Those who manned the human waves launched to clear minefields and to overpower Iraqi trenches were mostly young, untrained, and unarmed Iranian recruits to the Basij—the popular militia responsible for indoctrination, paramilitary training, and crowd control. These 20th-century Shi'a martyrs of the Iran-Iraq War became the symbols of the Revolution and an ideological rallying point. In the eyes of their commanding officers in the IRGC, the recruits repelled the advance of Iraq's forces and dislodged its soldiers from trenches and other fortifications during the long war of attrition. The fanatical zeal with which Iran sent its young into battle—not only with little chance of survival, but with the explicit purpose of seeking death as a tactic to overcome the enemy—revealed to the regime that indoctrination could greatly enhance a man's ability to defy natural survival instincts. As thousands upon thousands went willingly to their deaths, it occurred to Iran's leaders that such instruments could serve their purposes well beyond the killing fields of southern Iraq.

---

12   Algar, p. 200. The pretext for his speech was the announcement that Iran would mark 2,500 years of the Persian monarchy in what came to be an extravagant celebration held at Persepolis five years later. The speech is of critical importance for an understanding of Khomeini's and the Islamic Revolution's subversion of traditional Shi'a constructs of a just political order. It also offers the basis for the overthrow of Muslim rulers who do not subscribe to Khomeini's notion of Islamic governance.

From the human waves sent to clear minefields with the keys to heaven wrapped around their necks, the road to suicide terrorism in the name of fighting injustice was revealed. Soon after their arrival in Lebanon, IRGC representatives began to recruit locally among the Shi'a population. In a country devoured by years of ferocious sectarian warfare, it was not hard to find young men ready for battle. The IRGC offered a new ideology—along with enough money and weapons to supplant its more secular Sunni competitors in the sacred effort to fight Zionists and the West.

Before long, the Guards began advancing Iran's revolutionary agenda by challenging what they called "the forces of arrogance" on Mediterranean shores. Hezbollah targeted Israeli, U.S., and other Western targets, attacking its enemies with martyrdom operations and kidnappings.

The first recorded Hezbollah attack of this kind targeted an Israel Defense Forces headquarters in Tyre, Lebanon, on November 11, 1982, killing 75 Israeli soldiers and almost 30 Lebanese prisoners inside the compound at the time. Since then, Iran's Revolutionary Guards-trained proxies have made extensive use of suicide bombers, exporting their lethal menace to areas where they could kill their enemies in greater numbers. The Tyre attack was Hezbollah's maiden voyage, but it had a precedent—the bombing of the Iraqi embassy in downtown Beirut in December 1981, which killed 27 people and injured 100. The culprit was al-Dawa, another Iranian-backed Shi'a organization.[13]

In 1983, Hezbollah suicide bombers struck the U.S. Embassy in Beirut, killing 60; the barracks of the U.S. Marine peacekeepers in Beirut, killing 241; and the barracks of the French peace-keeping paratroopers, killing 63. In 1985, Iran-backed Hezbollah militants were responsible for kidnapping, torturing and murdering William Buckley, the CIA's chief of station in Beirut. Hezbollah was also responsible for hijacking TWA flight 847 and murdering an American passenger on board, U.S. Navy diver Robert Dean Stethem. In the midst of the hijacking, the attackers killed him and threw his body onto the tarmac of the Beirut airport. U.S. Marine Corps Lieutenant Colonel William R. Higgins met a similar fate three years later; in February 1988, Hezbollah kidnapped and murdered him while he served with the United Nations Truce Supervisory Organization (UNTSO) in southern Lebanon.

The new franchise spread even farther afield. In April 1988, a car bomb exploded outside a USO club in Naples, killing five, including one U.S. sailor, Angela Santos. A group called the Organization of Jihad Brigades, which the U.S. State Department considers an affiliate of Hezbollah, claimed responsibility for the attack. Responsibility was later

---

13  Assaf Moghadam, *The Globalization of Martyrdom.* (Baltimore, MD: Johns Hopkins University Press, 2008), p. 20.

EMANUELE OTTOLENGHI

attributed to the Japanese Red Army (JRA), which had a history of cooperating with Middle East terror groups and carrying out missions on their behalf, against a background of shared ideological grievances against the West.[14] That one of its members carried out the attack does not rule out the possibility of an Iranian-Hezbollah connection.

Iran's use of front organizations did not end in 1988. In the mid-1990s, a shadowy group called the Islamic Movement for Change claimed responsibility for two car bomb attacks on U.S. targets in Saudi Arabia. The first attack struck a U.S. military complex in Riyadh on November 13, 1995, killing five U.S. servicemen, and the second destroyed the Khobar Towers U.S. Air Force barracks in Dhahran on June 25, 1996, killing 19. Though some assume the Islamic Movement for Change to be an affiliate of al-Qaeda, other sources have linked it to Iran. In his 2008 book, *The Devil We Know*, former CIA case officer Robert Baer argues that Hezbollah's current leader, Hassan Nasrallah, complied with Iran's request to train the operatives who eventually carried out the attack.[15]

At the time, Osama bin Laden's franchise was based in Sudan, where it benefited from the help and training of Imad Mughniyah, Hezbollah's Lebanese terror mastermind.[16] Not only was Mughniyah the man behind the 1983 slaughter of U.S. soldiers and officials in Beirut, he also carried out the task of exporting Iran's newly developed martyrdom techniques to the Sunni world. He was dispatched to train al-Qaeda in the early 1990s and, in all likelihood, offered his advice to Hamas and the Palestinian Islamic Jihad when their leaderships were briefly stranded in South Lebanon in late 1992 as a result of a decision by Israel's late prime minister, Yitzhak Rabin, to deport 415 of their senior figures in response to a wave of terror attacks against Israeli civilians.[17] Contrary to the belief that Shi'a and Sunni fundamentalists are incapable of cooperating, the history of their relations shows a more complicated pattern, in which

---

14    According to the Federation of American Scientists' database, "The group had a history of close relations with Palestinian terrorist groups—based and operating outside Japan—since its inception…" The JRA carries responsibility for a number of attacks, including the 1972 Lod Airport massacre in Israel. One of its perpetrators, Kozo Okamoto, found refuge in Lebanon and was eventually granted political asylum there. According to the FAS, the JRA reportedly trained in Lebanon and Syria, making the Hezbollah connection plausible. See: www.fas.org/irp/world/para/jra.htm.

15    Robert Baer, *The Devil We Know*. (NY: Three Rivers Press, 2008), p. 163. Former FBI Director, Louis J. Freeh, claimed, in his memoirs, that the evidence trail pointed to Iran, but the Clinton Administration, then in power, did not wish to thwart prospects of rapprochement with the reformist Iranian President, Mohammad Khatami; see Louis J. Freeh, *My FBI Bringing Down the Mafia, Investigating Bill Clinton and Fighting the War on Terror*. (Waterville, ME: Thorndike Press, 2006). As Bruce Riedel commented in a recent U.S. Institute of Peace *Iran Primer* contribution that "Intelligence indicated the bombing was the work of Hezbollah al Hijaz, a Saudi Shiite group with close links to Iran's Revolutionary Guards and Lebanon's Hezbollah." See: http://iranprimer.usip.org/resource/clinton-administration.

16    Lawrence C. Wright, *The Looming Tower Al-Qaida and the Road to 9/11*. (NY: Alfred Knopf, 2006), p. 173.

17    No conclusive evidence exists of Mughniyah's personal involvement; regardless, the deepening of relations between Hamas, Palestinian Islamic Jihad and Iran date back to this same period. Such connections are discussed in the next pages.

fighters often set aside their hatreds and rivalries for tactical reasons to make common cause against shared enemies, not to mention the occasional doctrinal injunction (more frequent on the Shi'a side than among Sunni fundamentalists) to overcome divisions for the sake of Islam. This explains Osama bin Laden's decision to reach out to Hezbollah, and Hezbollah's decision to dispatch its leading terrorist to assist him in Sudan. It also explains Iran's steady, even if initially hesitant, support for the Palestinian Islamic Jihad and Hamas, which began in 1992 at the tune of $30 million a year, inclusive of military training, political assistance, the maintenance of both a Hamas and a Palestinian Islamic Jihad office in Tehran, and deepening ties that now go back at least 20 years.[18]

Iran's motivation in authorizing this kind of cooperation fits a pattern of Iranian support for Islamist movements across the Muslim world and the development of alliances that are sometimes alien to religious (but not necessarily ideological) doctrinal considerations. Whereas for Sunni fundamentalists, the Shi'a-Sunni schism is a theological one, and many Salafis view the Shi'a as apostates, the Iranian revolutionary view of this division is more political, centering on who leads the Community of the Faithful, and less focused on theological finer points. Such an approach, in a sense, reflects a pragmatism that often blends into Persian, rather than Islamic, national interest, Islamic rhetoric notwithstanding. Iranian support for Christian Armenia against Shi'a Azerbaijan during the war over Nagorno-Karabakh is a case in point. Iran's ambition is to reassert, in due course, Shi'a leadership in an Islamic revival that will unite Shi'a and Sunni in their struggle against the West. In this sense, the Islamic Revolution transcends the narrow confines of Shi'a Iranian Islam and seeks to assert itself as the leader of the downtrodden of the earth, whether Shi'a, Sunni or otherwise, against the arrogance of the Western world. As David Menashri notes:

> [F]rom the late 1960s Khomeini expressed ecumenical concepts. He considered the Iranian revolution a stage and an instrument in attaining Islamic unity (moral, if not political) and as a model for imitation by other Muslims... The concept of nationalism became alien to him, and he viewed it as an "imperialist plot" to divide and weaken Islam. Nationalism, he then claimed, was no better than tribal solidarity.[19]

---

18   Shaul Mishal & Avraham Sela, *The Palestinian Hamas: Vision, Violence and Coexistence*. (NY: Columbia University Press, 2000), pp. 97-98.

19   David Menashri, "Iran's Revolutionary Politics: Islam and National Identity," in Leonard Binder (Ed.), *Ethnic Conflict and International Politics in the Middle East*. (Gainesville, FL: The University Press of Florida, 1999), p. 134.

Providing training to al-Qaeda since the 1990s was therefore in keeping with Iran's revolutionary ideology of transcending borders and Islam's sectarian divide. This ecumenical impulse to paper over theological disputes so as to make common cause against infidel enemies had its mirror image in the Sunni world. As Lawrence Wright notes in his book, *The Looming Tower*, while discussing Osama bin Laden's Sudan period and his dealings with Sudanese Salafi ideologue Hasan al Turabi:

> Although bin Laden distrusted Turabi—hated him, even—he experimented with one of Turabi's most progressive and controversial ideas: to make common cause with Shi'ites... there was only one enemy now, the West, and the two main sects of Islam needed to come together to destroy it. Bin Laden invited Shiite representatives to speak to al-Qaeda, and he sent some of his top people to Lebanon to train with the Iranian-backed group Hezbollah. Imad Mugniyah, the head of Hezbollah's security service, came to meet bin Laden and agreed to train members of al-Qaeda in exchange for weapons.[20]

Wright notes how Hezbollah's successful mass murder of U.S. Marines and French paratroopers in Beirut "had made a profound impression on bin Laden, who saw that suicide bombers could be devastatingly effective and that, for all its might, America had no appetite for conflict."[21]

Though the Salafis had their own holy warriors and martyrs, they still lacked the means and the training to transform their murderous impulse into slaughter. Iran, its revolutionary emissaries, and its Lebanese proxies provided assistance and training that was then put to use with devastating effectiveness. The interaction between Hezbollah and the Salafists in Sudan enabled Osama bin Laden's ragtag army of holy warriors to dramatically upgrade their deadly skills and wreak havoc. Having learned the murderous art of high-powered explosives, suicide bombing, and synchronized martyrdom operations, al-Qaeda put its newly acquired skills to the cause of killing Americans. On August 7, 1998, al-Qaeda killed 212 and wounded 4,000 at the U.S. Embassy in Nairobi, and killed 11 and wounded 85 at the U.S. Embassy in Dar-es-Salaam. Two years later, on October 12, 2000, al-Qaeda attacked the U.S.S. Cole in the port of Aden in Yemen, killing 17 U.S. sailors and wounding 39. Finally, al-Qaeda struck the U.S. homeland itself on September 11, 2001.

---

20   Lawrence C. Wright, *The Looming Tower Al-Qaida and the Road to 9/11.* (NY: Alfred Knopf, 2006), p. 173.

21   *Ibid.* Wright also notes that contacts between al-Qaeda and Iran did not stop there but extended to training and financial assistance. The point of contact with Iran was Aiman al-Zawahiri, Osama bin Laden's Egyptian deputy who escaped Egypt after participating in the plot to assassinate the late Egyptian President, Anwar Sadat. According to Wright, Zawahiri's original interest in Iran stem from his study of the Iranian revolution and his hopes to apply that model to his home country.

This kind of cooperation was not limited to the training and transfer of expertise and know-how, nor was it limited to a specific period of time. As recently exposed by the U.S. Department of Treasury, Iran has allowed al-Qaeda to operate a network inside Iran for years. According to the U.S. Treasury, "This network serves as the core pipeline through which al-Qa'ida moves money, facilitators and operatives from across the Middle East to South Asia."[22]

Similarly, as previously noted, Hezbollah made its murderous techniques available to more than 400 Hamas and Palestinian Islamic Jihad leaders whom Israel had deported to southern Lebanon in December 1992, after a spat of knife and axe attacks against Israeli civilians in the preceding months. As Bruce Hoffman notes:

> During the nearly ten months they were in Lebanon, the Hamas exiles were able to establish the organization's first ties with Hezbollah. The PIJ, for its part, benefited doubly, forging tighter relations with Iran while significantly enhancing its military capabilities under Hezbollah's tutelage.[23]

Shaul Mishal and Avraham Sela further observe that:

> The deportation of 415 Islamic activists by Israel to Lebanon in December 1992 was a milestone in Hamas's decision to use car bombs and suicide attacks as a major *modus operandi* against Israel. Shortly afterwards, Hamas's leaders in Amman instructed its military activists to carry out two attacks, one by a car bomb, as a gesture to the deportees. Hamas's escalated military activity was an indirect result of the presence of the deportees for almost a year in south Lebanon, which provided the Palestinian Islamists an opportunity to learn about Hezbollah's experience in fighting the Israelis, the effect of suicide attacks, and the construction of car bombs.[24]

Once this cross-pollination took place, Iran's most original contribution to 20th-century terrorism was franchised to non-Shi'a, non-Persian terror organizations, with terrifying ripple effects.

---

22   "Treasury Targets Key Al-Qa'ida Funding and Support Network Using Iran as a Critical Transit Point," U.S. Department of Treasury Press Release, July 28, 2011, www.treasury.gov/press-center/press-releases/Pages/tg1261.aspx.

23   Bruce Hoffman, *Inside Terrorism*. (NY: Columbia University Press, 1999), p. 149.

24   Mishal & Sela, p. 66.

For Iran, there is a clear benefit. The cooperation with Sunni groups in the struggle against the West enabled Tehran to draw them to its own orbit and turn them into useful tools in its proxy war against Western influence. Additionally, it enabled Iran to credibly don the mantle of leader of the oppressed—thus fulfilling Khomeini's calling, whereby Iran's revolution transcends Persian-Arab, Sunni-Shi'a, and Muslim-Unbeliever divisions, and asserts itself as the new leader in the global efforts to resist the West. The Guards have proved to be a versatile tool for the fulfillment of this agenda.

Occasionally, the Iranian regime has sought to put its terror skills to use directly through its own operatives rather than its proxies. Iran was directly responsible for the 1992 bombing of the Israeli Embassy in Buenos Aires, which killed 29, and the Jewish communal organization AMIA in 1994, which killed 85, most of whom were Argentine nationals. Following the AMIA attack, Argentina's authorities issued an international arrest warrant for several Iranian officials, including then-president Akbar Hashemi Rafsanjani (until recently the chairman of the Assembly of Experts and of the Expediency Council), then-foreign minister Ali Akbar Velayati (currently the diplomatic adviser to the Supreme Leader), and then-Iranian Ambassador to Argentina Hadi Soleimanpour (currently the deputy minister for African Affairs at Iran's Ministry of Foreign Affairs). Interpol declined these three requests, but Argentina's warrants against the trio remain outstanding.

Interpol did, however, uphold warrants against several other Iranian officials involved in the plot: Ahmad Vahidi, Mohsen Rezai, Ali Fallahian, Mohsen Rabbani, and Ahmad Reza Asghari. At the time, Vahidi was commander of the Qods Forces. In 2007, he rose to the rank of deputy minister of defense and, in 2009, he became minister of defense. Rezai was the Revolutionary Guards' second commander and a presidential candidate in the 2009 presidential elections. Former intelligence minister Fallahian was the national security adviser to Iran's Supreme Leader, Ali Khamenei. Rabbani was cultural attaché at the Iranian Embassy in Argentina. Asghari also served at the Iranian Embassy at the time of the attack. Additionally, Interpol issued a related warrant for the arrest of Imad Mughniyah, who continued to mastermind Hezbollah's terrorist activities until his assassination in Damascus in February 2008.

In addition to its campaign of mass murder, Iran also dispatched the Guards to kill the regime's opponents in exile. The murder campaign to silence regime opponents was decided, ordered and carried out by the highest echelons of the regime:

Assassinations both at home and abroad were ordered directly by Ayatollah Khomeini while he was alive. After Khomeini's death, the responsibility for recommending individual assassinations fell to the Special Affairs Committee. Once the committee's recommendation was approved by the Supreme Leader, an individual committee member would be charged with implementing the decision with the assistance of the Ministry of Intelligence's Special Operations Council (*Shoray-e Amaliyat-e Vizheh*). The council's operational commanders received a written order signed by the Supreme Leader authorizing an assassination.[25]

The aforementioned Ali Fallahian, for example, is also wanted for several high-profile assassinations abroad, including that of Kazem Rajavi, the brother of slain MeK leader Massoud Rajavi, in Geneva in 1990 (for which Fallahian was convicted by a Swiss court). Iranian investigative reporter Akbar Ganjilater accused Fallahian of ordering the murders of prominent dissidents inside Iran.[26] Fallahian is also responsible for the murder of four Iranian Kurdish dissidents in the Mykonos restaurant attack in Berlin in 1992,[27] an episode that serves as an illustration of how the regime uses the IRGC against its enemies.

Once the decision to eliminate the Kurdish dissidents was taken, Fallahian assigned the task of carrying out the operation to Mohammad Hadi Hadavi Moghaddam, a Ministry of Intelligence officer who was in charge of the Kurdish opposition. He posed as the CEO of Samsam Kala, a Ministry of Intelligence company, to travel to Europe and gather intelligence. After Moghaddam filed his report and Germany was chosen as the location for the operation, Fallahian appointed two Ministry of Intelligence operatives to put the operation into place. They in turn recruited Kazem Darabi, an IRGC veteran who was living in Germany and had been active in the Union of Islamic Students' Associations of Europe, to carry out the operation. Darabi, for his part, chose the hit team by recruiting four individuals "who were known to him through their prior associations with Lebanese Shi'a militia groups Hezbollah and Amal."[28] The regime relied on the IRGC network abroad, on its connections to Hezbollah and Amal in Lebanon, and on commercial entities set up with the purpose of providing cover to carry out an assassination in the capital of a friendly country. In the judgment that sentenced Darabi to life for the massacre alongside his accomplice, Abdol-Rahman Banihashemi, the German court stated plainly that the regime had directly mandated the murder of its opponents and therefore issued an arrest warrant for Fallahian.[29]

---

25  *Murder at Mykonos: The Anatomy of a Political Assassination*, Iran Human Rights Documentation Center, 2007, www.iranomid.com/en/ARCHVS/murder_at_mykonos_report.pdf, p. 6.

26  Christopher De Bellaigue, "Cleric's Campaign Has Been Dogged by Murder Claims," *The Independent*, June 1, 2001, www.independent.co.uk/news/world/middle-east/clerics-campaign-has-been-dogged-by-murder-claims-686640.html.

27  For a detailed account of the Mykonos case and the trial that followed, see *Murder at Mykonos*.

28  *Ibid.*, p. 7.

29  *Ibid.*,p. 18.

EMANUELE OTTOLENGHI

Tehran's assassins have left behind a long trail of other high-profile deaths, including that of former Iranian Prime Minister Shahpour Bakhtiar, who was murdered in his Paris home in 1991. The list includes more than 100 prominent activists, former members of the Shah's army, civil service and political elites, and agitators from disparate opposition movements. More often than not, they met their deaths in Europe, where they thought they had found safe haven. Their assassins frequently managed to flee. Those who were caught were often acquitted or, as in the case with Darabi and Banihashemi, released early for political reasons.

The *Pasdaran*'s military role in the Islamic Republic is a reflection of their unflinching devotion to the Revolution and their loyalty to the Supreme Leader. Indeed, one of the reasons Yahia Rahim Safavi was replaced as chief commander of the IRGC in 2007 was that he had apparently become too openly sympathetic to President Mahmoud Ahmadinejad's policies. The current commander, Mohammad Ali Jafari, is thought to be very close to the Supreme Leader. But the enormous influence the Guards command, more than 30 years later, inside Iran's corridors of power, extends to the political and economic spheres as well. As Matthew Frick, a NATO senior officer, observes in a recent open source study on the IRGC:

> [I]t is evident that the key center of gravity in Iran is the Islamic Revolutionary Guard Corps (IRGC), or *Sepah-e Pasdaran* (Pasdaran). The IRGC's conventional military strength, uncompromising execution of its conceptual and constitutional mandates, political and economic influence, and direct as well as indirect control of the country's WMD programs combine to make the Pasdaran the source of the clerical regime's power both domestically and internationally.[1]

The most visible sign of this influence is the IRGC's presence in the country's high political offices. The Guards count many influential figures in government and public life among its former ranks.

Of the 21 cabinet members whom President Ahmadinejad submitted to the Majles for approval in September 2009, seven were former IRGC members, while many more have ties to the intelligence and security apparatus—a domain monopolized by the IRGC. They hold key positions as ministers in the Ministries of Commerce, Defense, Economics, Intelligence, Interior, Islamic Guidance, and Oil. In the previous cabinet,

---

1    Matthew M. Frick, "Iran's Islamic Revolutionary Guard Corps: An Open Source Analysis," *Joint Force Quarterly*, Issue 49, 2nd Quarter, 2008, www.dtic.mil/cgi-bin/GetTRDoc?Location=U2&doc=GetTRDoc.pdf&AD=ADA516529, p. 121.

which served from 2005 to 2009, the Guards held even more positions, but key ministries remained in the hands of their trusted former officers and comrades.[2]

Reportedly, a third of the Majles is made up of former members of the IRGC, including its Speaker Ali Larijani. Many deputy ministers are also former IRGC members, as are a growing number of provincial governors.[3]

Larijani's successor as head of the Supreme Council for National Security, Dr. Saeed Jalili, is a former Guard.

The current chief of the Armed Forces General Staff, Brigadier General Hassan Firouzabadi, is a senior member of the IRGC—thus effectively placing the *Artesh* under IRGC command. This is not a new development, as one of Firouzabadi's predecessors, Ali Shamkhani, was also a *Pasdar*, but it demonstrates the general trend of "Pasdaranization" in Iran's power structures.

This is not to say that former IRGC members all act as a disciplined political party. There are rivalries and divisions that are both personal and ideological.[4] There is considerable discussion among experts and scholars about the extent to which the presence of IRGC members in positions of power reflects IRGC influence.

---

2    Roozbeh Shafshekhan & Farzan Sabet, "The Ayatollah's Praetorians: The Islamic Revolutionary Guard Corps and the 2009 Election Crisis," *The Middle East Journal,* Vol. 64, No. 4, Autumn 2010, p. 553: "Today there are members of the IRGC and related organizations directly entering political office. The new Ahmadinejad cabinet is a case in point, in that nearly every appointee has direct or very strong security establishment ties, with only a single clergyman. Mostafa Mohammad Najjar, the Interior Minister, is the ex-Minister of Defense and before that was a top IRGC commander. General Ahmad Vahidi, the Defense Minister, was Deputy Defense Minister in the last Ahmadinejad government and before that the commander of the IRGC Quds Force. Heydar Moslehi, the Intelligence Minister, was Khamenei's representative in the IRGC Ground Force and Basij Resistance Force and before that Khomeini's representative in the *Kerbala* and *Khatim al-Anbiya' Headquarters* during the Iran-Iraq war. Masoud Mirkazemi, Oil Minister, was head of ETKA in the Ministry of Defense. Reza Taqipoor, Communications and Information Technology Minister, was head of Shiraz Electronic Industries where he founded the electronic warfare research division. These are just obvious examples of the militarization of a hitherto civilian and clerical government."

3    Greg Bruno, *Iran's Revolutionary Guards*, Council of Foreign Relations' Backgrounder, June 22, 2009, www.cfr.org/iran/irans-revolutionary-guards/p14324.

4    Jerry Guo, "Letter from Tehran: Iran's New Hardliners," *Foreign Affairs*, September 30, 2009, www.foreignaffairs.com/features/letters-from/letter-from-tehran-irans-new-hard-liners: "Until recently, the IRGC was split between pragmatists and hard-liners. In 2001, three-quarters of the IRGC's 130,000 foot soldiers voted to reelect Khatami. At least one internal government poll before this summer's election showed that a "high percentage" of the IRGC's rank and file planned to vote for Mousavi. Four days before the election, the organization's weekly newspaper, the *Sobh-e Sadeq*, warned of a "Velvet Green revolution" and promised that the IRGC would not allow the opposition to triumph. Then, immediately following the polls, IRGC commanders purged leaders who were sympathetic to the reformists, leaving a united bloc of hard-liners whose views lie at the extreme right."

However, the rise of the IRGC as a powerful political player is not in dispute.[5]

How did a revolutionary militia come to be the main political and economic player of this clerical dominated regime?

There were strong factors both for and against the rise of the *Pasdaran* in Iran's politics. The Guards had shown uncommon sacrifice and considerable military ingenuity in the war. They had fought on all fronts and, alongside the Basiji, had often been on the frontlines both as crack troops and cannon fodder. Their devotion to the Revolution, compared to the *Artesh*'s past involvement with the Shah, was an additional advantage, for it guaranteed loyalty to the regime from a well-armed force that, unlike the regular army, could always be trusted.

Against the Guards, by contrast, stood the plain fact of a country exhausted by a pointless war, whose futile continuation, at least past 1982, only the regime's obduracy had guaranteed. Theirs was the fanaticism that led tens of thousands of young Iranians to an untimely and cruel death while the *Artesh* had regularly counseled against the kind of military adventures an under-equipped Iran could not hope to ever decisively win. Then there was the Guards' decision, late in the war, to expand the conflict into the Persian Gulf.

In 1988, when Khomeini reluctantly ended the Iran-Iraq war, the IRGC was at the nadir of its influence, after a long and bloody stalemate with Saddam and a brief but humiliating defeat at the hands of the United States. Specifically, as Stephen R. Ward writes, the second Guards' commander, Mohsen Rezai, was "publicly disgraced" in 1988, "when he was forced to... take responsibility" for one of the worst military defeats Iran incurred during the war.[6]

Other factors played against the Guards. Logic and circumstances counseled in favor of merging the two militaries, especially as a devastated economy required that defense resources be spent wisely on rearmament and improving military capability. These were strong arguments against maintaining two parallel armies. Additionally, the Guards' excess of zeal, which had cost the country so much, began to come under

---

5    Shafshekhan and Sabet, in particular, identify a group, within the Guards, which they call neo-principalists, as being the engine behind the IRGC rise as a political powerhouse inside Iran: "The Neo-Principalist ideology has key features that distinguish it from other factions in the IRI. Their political ideology is influenced by the jurisprudence of Ayatollah Mohammad Taqi Mesbah-Yazdi, though despite its outward veneer of Islamic fundamentalism, it has strong anti-clerical, authoritarian, nationalistic, and pragmatic tendencies. The resulting doctrine has strong parallels with the Chinese model, being politically authoritarian with a strong emphasis on economic development, national independence, and grandeur." Shafshekhan & Sabet, p. 550.

6    Ward, p. 301.

scrutiny within the ranks of the regime. But the Guards would not give up without a fight; they marched fully armed through Tehran at the end of the Iran-Iraq War to prevent authorities from daring to merge the two armed services and imposing strict supervision over them. This display of force and the open challenge it represented to the regime achieved its goal. Though the country was weary of war and revolution, the IRGC succeeded in preserving itself as a pillar of national defense expanding its role in the fabric of the state. In fact, it gained pre-eminence in Iran's dual defense structure and, with the reforms that the armed services underwent after the war, consolidated its role as both a defender and an exporter of the revolution.[7]

In time, the Iranian government delivered some of its most sophisticated weaponry to the IRGC military branches. It also charged the IRGC with expanding and dramatically improving its existing indigenous arms industry. Iran had learned one lesson from the Iran-Iraq war: an isolated country needs to rely on its own production capabilities to meet future threats. This lesson included responsibility for developing Iran's ballistic missile and nuclear weapons programs. The IRGC also strengthened its ability to guarantee order against anti-government sedition at home. This capability was greatly enhanced by the gradual integration of the Basij militia into its command structure.

The rise to new heights of power was not without challenge. Under Ali Akbar Hashemi Rafsanjani's presidency, between 1989 and 1997, technocrats tasked with reconstruction were more mindful than in the previous decade of the limits of Iran's power abroad. Haunted by the costs of rebuilding a war-ravaged country, they exercised more caution in pursuing confrontations with the West. Rafsanjani's presidency thus encouraged the Guards to branch out into the economy, so as to ensure independent sources of financing for their military and overseas activities at a time when state coffers were strapped for cash. But it also kept the Guards close and took care to keep them loyal by consolidating their military primacy and ensuring that an expanding economic presence would address the aspirations of their veterans.

Greater caution did not mean an abandonment of early revolutionary commitments; the regime remained well anchored in the Islamic worldview of its founders. Since the early days of the Revolution, two Islamic souls have vied for power in Iran: the Islamic left and the Islamic right. Their fault lines, originally, had to do more with socio-economic outlooks than with clerical rule. Both groups counted influential

---

7    Ironically, then President Ali Akhbar Hashemi Rafsanjani opened the gates to the IRGC's involvement in Iran's economy as a way to check the Guards' power after the war. Twenty years later, one cannot but notice how his efforts not only ended in failure, but in fact backfired.

EMANUELE OTTOLENGHI

clerics in their ranks and their respective strength left the political system frequently paralyzed in the 1980's. Since the end of the Iran-Iraq war and Khomeini's death, power shifted decisively to the more conservative right, thanks especially to the elevation of Seyyed Ali Khamenei as Iran's new Supreme Leader. In time, the left evolved and moved away from an unflinching commitment to clerical oversight of the state.

The events leading to Khomeini's succession also contributed to the transformation of the *Pasdaran* into the power behind the throne. Khamenei had impeccable revolutionary and political credentials. As a young seminary student and follower of Khomeini, he had been arrested in the 1963 Qom disturbances. As noted, he narrowly escaped a 1981 assassination attempt that left him permanently impaired, and soon after, a staggering 95 percent majority elected him president. Though no one could doubt Khamenei's revolutionary *bona fides*, his credentials as a religious cleric, learned jurisprudent, and source of spiritual emulation were insufficient for the office that he stood to hold. Besides, until a few weeks before Khomeini's death, another, much more prominent cleric, was slated to fill the highest office in the land—Grand Ayatollah Ali Montazeri.

Not all Shi'a clerics, including some very senior figures, accept the principle of *velayat-e faqih* as it developed in practice under Khomeini's and later Khamenei's stewardship. Though Montazeri, Khomeini's student and presumed successor until 1989, embraced the concept in his younger years, later in life he came to believe that the legitimacy of the *Faqih* ultimately came from the people, and had grown increasingly alarmed by the events inside Iran, where large-scale injustices were occurring in the name of Islamic governance. Having voiced publicly his discomfort at a ferocious wave of repression against political prisoners, thousands of whom were summarily executed in the fall of 1988, Montazeri was defrocked and consigned to house arrest for the rest of his life, as an example for those who might dare challenge the system.[8] Against the background of Montazeri's demise, Khomeini apparently designated Khamenei as his successor,[9] and in order to remove the legal impediments that existed in the Iranian constitution to such a junior

---

8    Moin, p. 279. Also, according to Foundation for Defense of Democracies Senior Fellow Reuel Marc Gerecht, "Fallen from power, Montazeri wrote a six-volume critique of the *velayat-e faqih*... which allowed first Khomeini, then Khamenei, dictatorial control of the state. Although Montazeri never took issue with the idea that clerics should have an important role in government, he relentlessly pursued Khamenei for his lack of religious qualifications and for the very idea that the supreme leader is unelected and not subject to law and tradition. For Montazeri, the Islamic Republic was born in sin because the *velayate faqih* was not prescribed by Shiite tradition." See Reuel Marc Gerecht, "Going Rogue —Hossein Ali Montazeri, 1922-2009," *The Weekly Standard*, January 4, 2010, Vol. 15, No. 16, www.weeklystandard. com/Content/Public/Articles/000/000/017/390wrflv.asp.

9    Moin, p. 287.

ranking cleric, he ordered a constitutional revision that could install Khamenei in the Supreme Leader's chair.[10]

Constitutionally, the Supreme Leader was meant to be defined, according to Khomeini, by mastery of Islamic jurisprudence as well as the belief that a cleric should be at the helm of state—plus loyalty to Khomeini. Khamenei's personal loyalty to him, to the Revolution, and to *velayat-e faqih* thus combined the three principal qualities Khomeini sought in a successor. Other more senior and venerable clerics lived in Iran at the time, but none met all three criteria.

In acceding to the role of Supreme Leader, Khamenei would have to rule over his clerical peers, and command their abiding loyalty. However, because of his theological deficiencies, he could not fully rely on the clerical class. Though a powerful politician, Khamenei was still a relatively junior cleric, with little scholarly stature and, lacking Khomeini's charisma and his religious authority, he was inclined to turn elsewhere for his sources of influence and power. The Guards were an obvious choice for him. His first post after the Revolution had been deputy defense minister. Then, as wartime president, he had shown a keen interest in military matters and spent time strengthening his ties with the Guards. Once Leader, he cemented his relations with the IRGC by posting his own personal representatives to the Guards. There is no evidence that a formal agreement existed under which the Guards would guarantee the Supreme Leader's enduring rule in exchange for his protection and his support in political and economic matters.[11] But their oath of loyalty, and the assurance that Khamenei would not condone any attempt by Iran's political forces to stray from Khomeini's path, guaranteed their support. Khamenei, for his part, increasingly relied on their loyalty to maintain his grip on power.

This bond between the Guards and the Leader meant that, during the Rafsanjani presidency, the stronger emphasis on reconstruction at home and improvement of

---

10 *Ibid.*, p. 293: "Khomeini had already made it known to his inner circle that Ali Khamenei was now his favored candidate for succession. In religious terms, however, Khamenei was too junior and his scholarly qualifications insufficient for even the ingenious strategists who surrounded the Imam to find a way to have him declared a *marja*. On Khomeini's own instructions, therefore, Article 109 of the constitution requiring that the leader should be a *marja-e taqlid* was removed, as were the provisions that allowed, in the absence of a single, qualified individual, for a collegiate leadership."

11 See for example Mehdi Khalaji, "Militarization of the Iranian Judiciary," *Policy Watch 1567*, Washington Institute for Near East Policy, August 13, 2009, http://washingtoninstitute.org/templateC05.php?CID=3105. Khalaji argues that "in his twenty years in office, particularly in recent years, Khamenei has replaced military, political, economic, cultural, and clerical officials with a new generation of politicians and clerics who owe their political or religious credentials to him. The IRGC and intelligence apparatuses became the main avenues through which young ambitious men loyal to Khamenei could enter the political scene. Although most of these new politicians and clerics are close to Khamenei, they are not traditional clerics with independent political and religious credentials, such as those who participated in the 1979 Revolution. Instead, most of the new generation began their careers in the military, the IRGC, and the intelligence services."

relations abroad would not come at the expense of the Revolution. The Guards were given ample proof of that through both the largesse of economic contracts funneled to the IRGC's construction company *Khatam al-Anbiya*—a conglomerate currently headed by IRGC officer Abolqasem Mozaffari Shams—and the continuation of certain aspects of foreign policy—support for radical Islamic movements abroad and the targeting of dissidents—would contnue.

The threat posed briefly by Montazeri to the system, however, did not go away. The left, briefly sidelined politically during the Rafsanjani presidency (1989-1997), refashioned itself as the reformist movement and came back with a vengeance in 1997, when Mohammad Khatami won by a landslide in the presidential elections. Reformists sought gradual change within the framework of Islamic governance, including crucially more individual freedoms and a less confrontational approach with the West in foreign policy. On both accounts, their agenda appeared to imperil the IRGC's worldview, power, and policies, and was regularly met with confrontation and violence.[12]

Under Khatami's reformist presidency, from 1997 to 2005, it appeared, at least briefly, that the modest openings the government had authorized to the West might breach the ideological ramparts the Guards had erected around the Revolution. A new atmosphere of limited freedom reigned in Iran, as attested by the relaxation in press restrictions that led to a media spring of sorts. But it was short-lived. The IRGC did not appreciate the signs of change. The first indication that Khatami would be forced to bow to the IRGC occurred on July 9, 1999, when paramilitary forces stormed student dormitories at the University of Tehran to crush demonstrations protesting the closure of the reformist daily newspaper, *Salam*. Though the trigger had been the newspaper closure, the demonstrations were about much more than that—and the Guards saw the students' stirrings as a clear sign of subversion and as evidence that, with newly found freedoms, ordinary Iranians would openly challenge the very foundations of the Islamic Republic's system of governance. Having obtained the green light from the Supreme Leader to quell the protests, the IRGC went on the offensive and very publicly expressed its resolution to prevent reformist policies from running their course. In an open letter to president Khatami in the conservative daily *Kayhan* on July 19, 1999, two-dozen senior officers in the IRGC hinted ominously that the reformist course was undermining the Revolution:

> In the aftermath of recent events, and in our capacity as servants since the days of the Holy Defense of the noble Iranian nation, we deem it our

---

12  Khatami was proverbially nicknamed 'Ayatollah Gorbachev' by his detractors—someone whose commitment to gradual reforms nevertheless ends up undermining the system at its foundations. See John Lancaster, "Khatemi, Iran's Ayatollah Gorbachev," *The Washington Post*, May 25, 1997, p. A29.

duty to bring certain matters before your learned and worthy Excellency. We hope that in your magnanimity, and in keeping with your worthy credo, and in consonance with the path which you promote (to hear all speech and ideas though they be contrary), that you [will address] this matter which may reflect the worries of thousands who have suffered for the Revolution and who today—without any political partisanship—look upon the troubles of the Revolution with a nervous eye, and who are perplexed and bewildered by the silence, negligence, and naïveté of officials who have gained their positions by virtue of the blood of thousands of martyrs... our patience is at an end, and we do not think it possible to tolerate any more if [this matter is] not addressed.[13]

The regime got the message: Khatami's openings had gone too far and it was time to roll back the freedom carpet. The government suffocated the student protests and the liberalizing national media with a campaign of bloody repression, which was repeatedly unleashed for the remainder of Khatami's two-term presidency. With the reformists in retreat, there was little standing in the way of the IRGC's path to assert its influence over Iran's political system and, in the process, kill whatever remained of the Khatami era's modest reformist impulse.

In 2003, the IRGC, then still under the command of General Yahya Rahim Safavi, entered politics through local elections, marking a decisive turn of events in Iranian politics, and ensuring that what it saw as a reformist threat could not reconstitute itself. Having conquered the Majles a year later, in 2005, with the full knowledge of the Supreme Leader, the Guards backed the hardline, populist mayor of Tehran, Mahmoud Ahmadinejad, for the presidency. According to the aforementioned RAND report:

> Beginning first with its episodic confrontations against reform activists during the Khatami era, networks of active and former IRGC officers began to take on an increasingly political role that enabled the IRGC—by design or by accident—to emerge as a sort of "guardian" for conservatives seeking to displace Khatami supporters from political power. In 2003, former IRGC members or associates took control of numerous city and town councils, paving the way for their entry into legislative politics during the 2004 parliamentary elections. Of 152 new members elected to the Majles in February 2004, 91 had IRGC backgrounds, and a further 34 former IRGC officers now hold senior-level posts in the government.

---

13   The letter appeared in Kayhan, on July 19, 1999. It is available, in English translation, at www.iranian.com/News/1999/July/irgc.html.

EMANUELE OTTOLENGHI

During the June 2005 presidential elections, besides Ahmadinejad, there were three other candidates associated with the IRGC.[14]

Though it is unclear whether Ahmadinejad was himself a *Pasdar* during the early days of the Revolution, as some sources claim, or a Basij militia member, his political sympathies undoubtedly were with the more hardline elements of the regime, including the senior ranks of the IRGC. His ideology is also at home with the Islamist fervor of those among the Guards and their conservative backers in the regime, who loath the reformist trend toward greater individual freedoms and accommodation with the West, and aspire instead to return Iran to its revolutionary roots.

The IRGC further consolidated its grip on power when most reformist candidates were disqualified from participating in the 2008 parliamentary elections, paving the way to a Majles takeover by conservative politicians. But with the 2009 presidential elections looming, reformers mounted another challenge. The popular unrest surrounding the 2009 presidential contest offered a pretext to corner the left and to give the reformist movement the proverbial coup de grace. While before 2009 neither side questioned the founding principles of the Islamic Republic, the Islamic right has routinely accused the left of not being loyal enough to the Supreme Leader. Conservative forces close to the Supreme Leader and the President detected evidence in the opposition's outcry that the elections were fraudulently fixed, that the reformists were "deviant." In other words, they had betrayed the Revolution.

In 2009, the left fielded two candidates with pristine revolutionary credentials—the war-time former prime minister, Mir-Hossein Mousavi (1981-1989), and the cleric and former Majles Speaker Mehdi Karroubi (1989-1992 and 2000-2004)—both veterans of the Revolution. Mousavi in particular stirred the crowds and galvanized a reformist camp that had, by then, resigned itself to apathy and abstention in the rigged voting charade of Iranian elections. Until June 11, the eve of the elections, Mousavi was the frontrunner. When the regime hastily announced that the incumbent president, Mahmoud Ahmadinejad, had won a sweeping victory, Iranians took peacefully to the streets to protest and demanded a recount.[15] Yet, no matter how peaceful the protests were, the IRGC saw them as a threat to the regime's survival and evidence that a dark conspiracy was at play. Yadollah Javani, the head of IRGC's office of political affairs—the directorate tasked with indoctrination—had warned reformists a day before the elections that the IRGC would not tolerate a "velvet revolution" and ominously said that such an occurrence would be "nipped in the

---

14    Frederic Wherley et al., *The Rise of the Pasdaran*, RAND Corporation, 2009, p. 77.

15    For an account and analysis of Iran's post-election crisis, see Ali Ansari, *Crisis of Authority: Iran's 2009 Presidential Elections.* (Washington, D.C.: Chatham House, 2010).

bud."[16] It was. As protests mounted, the regime unleashed its security forces, under the leadership of the IRGC and its commander, General Ali Jafari, to crush the demonstrators before their demands could reach a full-scale assault on the regime's legitimacy.

Eventually, the 2009 post-election wave of repression radicalized supporters of reform, pushing them to openly demand the demise of the Islamic Republic's founding system of government. Other cracks started to appear; clerics began to voice unprecedented public criticism and, when the late Ali Montazeri passed away in late 2009, his funeral became a catalyst for more dissent. With the very foundations of the Islamic Republic under assault, the IRGC led the struggle alongside those clerics from the right who still upheld Khomeini's vision. As with their direct interference with the student movement in 1999, ten years later the Guards saw Mousavi's candidacy and the coalition backing him as a threat to the system of government they have sworn to uphold. As in the past, domestic challenges to the regime were suffocated in bloody repressions—and the net result has been that the repressive apparatus and its loyal executioners have become more entrenched in the system.

Two years later, though the embers of revolt are still burning, it appears that the Islamic Republic has survived yet another challenge. Regardless, more tensions are surfacing—surprisingly perhaps, among former allies in the Islamic right. General Jafari and his Revolutionary Guards, yet again, may be called to determine the fate and future of those in the fight.

Ahmadinejad's election was a triumph against reformists, and it may have represented an effort to return Iran to its early revolutionary fervor, but the challenge to the rule of the Jurisprudent does not necessarily come only from the left and among the clerics. Ahmadinejad and his associates embrace a fundamentalist view of Islam—one that may seek to bypass the clerics' intermediary role between man and God. He is the first non-clerical figure to accede to the office of the presidency since the early days of the Revolution—no secular leader has held the office since 1981.[17] This is a significant development for a theocracy founded on the principle of clerical rule, and it may be a harbinger of change—though what sort and how much remain in question.

---

16   Quoted in Thomas Erdbrink, "Rallies Close out Iranian Campaign," *The Washington Post*, June 11, 2009, www.washingtonpost.com/wp-dyn/content/article/2009/06/10/AR2009061003548_pf.html.

17   There were two non-clerical presidents in Iran prior to Khamenei's hasty election in 1981—Abolhassan Bani-Sadr and Mohammad-Ali Rajai. Bani-Sadr won the first presidential election after Khomeini's frontrunner, Jalaleddin Farsi, was forced to withdraw on a technicality late in the campaign. Bani-Sadr only lasted until June 1981 when he was impeached and forced to go into exile. His successor, Rajai died in a MeK terror attack on August 30, 1981 and was succeeded by Khamenei, a cleric. Since then, and until Ahmadinejad, only clerics served in the highest elected state office of the Islamic Republic of Iran.

EMANUELE OTTOLENGHI

Many of Iran's revolutionary leaders who are unflinchingly loyal to the *velayat-e faqih* are not clerics—and herein lies the problem for the IRGC and its political allies. The Islamic Republic's legitimacy rests on the principle of clerical rule, but the powerful combination of religious and revolutionary fervor lies with lay leaders who rose through the ranks of the IRGC, the intelligence and the military. Ahmadinejad's access to the highest elected office in Iran, coupled with the spreading influence of his non-clerical (but devotedly Islamist) allies, could signal a shift, which the current Supreme Leader may bless, exploit to stay in power, or seek to quash, lest it mounts a challenge to the Islamic order he presides over.

The rise of lay leaders, intent on restoring the fervor of the early days of the Revolution, may thus end up fending off a reformist challenge to the Supreme Leader by sidelining the religious establishment altogether[18]—something that has triggered a backlash against President Ahmadinejad in the early months of 2011. As he entered the last two years of his second term, an acute dispute erupted between Ahmadinejad and Khamenei over the continued cabinet presence of Heydar Moslehi, the minister of intelligence and former Supreme Leader's representative with the IRGC. This is a struggle among hardliners—not over God's rule or even reforms. Ultimately, the Guards, under Ali Jafari's command, will determine who wins.

The end of clerical rule could spell the end of the Islamic Republic, something that the Guards will not tolerate. As with the challenge from the left, the IRGC is likely to side with the Supreme Leader and fulfill its calling, even if the power struggle it is asked to settle involves an erstwhile ally who rewarded it handsomely for its services.[19]

Ahmadinejad's election opened the door for a gradual takeover by former IRGC loyalists of key government and elected positions. The reformist challenge of 2009 increased the political weight of the Guards and confirmed their critical role as gatekeepers of the regime's inner sanctum. With the reformist threat momentarily at bay and a power struggle under way between the Supreme Leader and a president who emerged with the backing of the IRGC political faction, the IRGC may expand its political role even further to settle the clash and, in the process, emerge ever more powerful. Indeed, the IRGC remains the final arbiter of power and, as with the original Praetorians in Roman times, a king maker in Iranian politics.

---

18   Shafshekhan & Sabet, p. 553.

19   According to Jerry Guo, "During his presidency in the early 1990s, Rafsanjani steered oil development projects to family and friends. In 2005, Ahmadinejad defeated Rafsanjani and promised to take on the "oil mafia"—but then loaded two-thirds of his cabinet with IRGC veterans, signed off on hundreds of no-bid construction and petrochemical contracts for IGRC-backed companies, and condoned the IRGC's proliferating smuggling networks, which net $12 billion a year, according to one Iranian lawmaker." See Jerry Guo, "Letter from "Tehran: Iran's New Hardliners," *Foreign Affairs*, September 30, 2009, www.foreignaffairs.com/features/letters-from/letter-from-tehran-irans-new-hard-liners.

# CHAPTER 5: THE IRGC CONQUEST OF IRAN'S ECONOMY

The IRGC's increased political influence since the late 1980s has helped consolidate another trend—the IRGC's permeation of Iran's economy—where its power is no less impressive.

The interaction among military, economic and political power is critical in understanding the centrality of the IRGC to Iran's current system; the IRGC takes advantage of its influence and capabilities in one realm in order to increase its involvement in another. Its growing economic clout is both an end in and of itself and a tool to advance other agendas. Thus, IRGC revenues from economic activities yield political leverage and the resources needed to advance its loyal members in positions of power. Its power, conversely, serves the economic enterprises it owns. But the profits inevitably fund its military activities, its involvement in the procurement and development efforts in the nuclear and ballistic missile programs—which in turn enhance its prestige and power within the system. Meanwhile, the Guards' growing political and economic influence enables them to bank on the willingness of public companies to lend their services—both at home and abroad—to aid in the Guards' efforts to procure forbidden technologies and raw materials, and to finance their purchases through middlemen on foreign markets.

As noted before, the IRGC is not a monolith—many of its veterans are not necessarily aligned with the hardliners at the top. The Guards' transition from military force to a business empire may have also sowed the seeds of new divisions because of economic competition. A RAND report on the IRGC, *The Rise of the Pasdaran*, noted in 2009:

> [T]he IRGC's expansion into the business sector harnessed the informal social networks that had developed among veterans and former officials. Thus, when we describe the IRGC's economic influence, we use a very broad definition, that captures the informality of its reach.[1]

In other words, one cannot assume that the many economic vehicles the IRGC, under the command of General Jafari, has come to control will always act in unison, or

---

[1]    Wherley et al., p. 56.

that a guardsman will follow a centralized or coordinated strategy to serve a political purpose. The IRGC's diversification into the Iranian economy necessarily produced rivalries and gave rise to businesses conducted purely for the sake of self-enrichment. The same, incidentally, can be said of the Soviet Communist Party bureaucracy and the infighting that occurred at the Politburo.

Nevertheless, in building a commercial empire, the IRGC has conflated its founding mission—regime survival—with its own pecuniary appetites.

The IRGC's economic prowess began, much like its political trajectory, at the end of the Iran-Iraq War in 1988. The end of the war demobilized masses of young men looking for jobs. For the regime, the battle-hardened veterans returning home to a country devastated by years of war, centralized economic planning, and political isolation constituted a tremendous challenge but also an opportunity. The IRGC had made its recruits and young officers all members of the rising elites of Iran's new order. Their high levels of indoctrination guaranteed loyalty. Their uniform and service provided them a place in the ranks of the Revolution, but also skills and access to education, especially once the thorough process of purges and indoctrination had guaranteed that university faculties were Islamicized enough that the Regime could afford, in the midst of the Iran-Iraq War, to reopen them without running the risk of a countercoup from students and intellectuals. Fighting a war over eight years had required the Guards to develop a corps of engineers with advanced technical skills in building tunnels, trenches, pontoons and other projects, and it now enabled them to release thousands of trained engineers into the labor market.

With the end of hostilities, these engineers could now devote themselves to reconstruction. Iran's constitution was vague about the role of the *Pasdaran* in guarding the Revolution and its achievements, but their responsibilities did not have to be limited to policing and fighting alone. Besides, as analyst Ali Alfoneh notes,[2] article 147 of the constitution states:

> In time of peace, the government must utilize the personal and technical equipment of the Army in relief operations, and for educational and productive ends, and the Construction Jihad, while fully observing the criteria of Islamic justice and ensuring that such utilization does not harm the combat-readiness of the Army...[3]

---

2    See Ali Alfoneh, "How Intertwined Are the Revolutionary Guards in Iran's Economy?" *AEI Middle Eastern Outlook*, October 22, 2007, www.irantracker.org/analysis/how-intertwined-are-revolutionary-guards-irans-economy.

3    The full English text of the Islamic Republic of Iran's Constitution is available at www.iranonline.com/iran/iran-info/government/constitution-9-3.html.

Building infrastructure and bringing progress to the far corners of Iran's vast and underdeveloped hinterlands served the goals of the Revolution, and Iran's leaders hoped it would keep the citizenry loyal to their ideals much in the same way that it does elsewhere in the world of both Shi'a and Sunni Islamists—by building roads, schools and hospitals in the name of the Revolution. Rebuilding the country became a duty no less sacred than defending its soil. Soon after the war's end, Rafsanjani enacted a presidential decree establishing the IRGC's Construction Base of the Seal of the Prophets, a.k.a. *Gharargah Sazandegi-ye Khatam-al-Anbiya*, also known as *Khatam-al-Anbiya* or *Ghorb*. *Ghorb*'s specific task is to reconstruct the country and its economy in the spirit of its revolutionary ideals. Thus began the Guards' remarkable journey to the economic empire they are today.

The IRGC indirectly controls two economic conglomerates that are unique to Iran's revolutionary structures: the Foundation of the Oppressed of the Earth (*Bonyad-e Mostazafan*) and the Foundation of Martyrs and Veterans' Affairs (*Bonyad-e Shahid va-Omur-e-Janbazan*). The immensely lucrative and influential Foundation of the Oppressed has extensive business interests across Iran's economy. According to Alfoneh, the Foundation is "an independent financial body traditionally run by a retired IRGC commander and used by the state as a proxy to fund off-the-books IRGC operations."[4] The current director of the Foundation, Mohammad Forouzandeh, is a former IRGC officer. The same applies to the Foundation for Martyrs' and Veteran Affairs, currently headed by former IRGC Air Force commander Hossein Dehghan. The Foundation acts as a mortgage lender to Basijis' and martyrs' families, and as an influential stakeholder in Iran's economy.[5]

Given the frequently opaque nature of the IRGC, it is hard to quantify the combined value of all contracts for which IRGC companies successfully bid. Still, credible estimates suggest the IRGC controls anywhere between 25 and 40 percent of Iran's GDP—the equivalent of tens of billions of dollars.[6] If one considers that its share of Iran's GDP in 1989 was around 5 percent, it becomes clear how remarkable the IRGC's expansion as an economic force has been, both in relative and absolute terms.

---

4    Alfoneh, "How Intertwined Are the Revolutionary Guards in Iran's Economy?"

5    The complete list of companies controlled by the Foundation of the Oppressed can be found on its website: www.irmf.ir/en/EN-RelatedCompanies.aspx.

6    See Elliot Hen-Tov and Nathan Gonzalez, "The Militarization of Post-Khomeini Iran: Praetorianism 2.0," *The Washington Quarterly*, Vol. 34, No. 1, Winter 2011, pp. 45-59. This is how Hen-Tov and Nathan Gonzalez explain their estimate (footnote 29, page 58): "one can infer the total value of all entities subordinate to the Guard or a member of the Guard network by the use of proxy data—the revenue of Guard companies and subsidiaries, estimates of illicit smuggling revenues based on trade discrepancies, newly-acquired assets in the recent wave of privatizations, and control of parastatal assets through Guard veterans. Adding the above components together, the Guards appear to exercise some form of control over at least 25 percent at the lower range and up to 40 percent of GDP at the higher range of estimates."

The Foundation for the Oppressed, established after the Revolution to take over government assets associated with the Shah and his regime, is an especially powerful economic force in Iran and its special status affords it significant benefits.

Among its assets are several key national industries. The Foundation has a stake in Iran's mining, food and beverage, agriculture and animal husbandry, trade and transport, civil development and housing, tourism and recreational centers, real estate, and energy industries.

Its companies engage in improving productivity, establishing new companies, and participating in both domestic and international investments. Its subsidiaries produce tires, natural and synthetic fibers, lubricants, wood, cellulose, metal products, textile and garment material, motorcycles, refrigerators and freezers, iron and aluminum, tile and ceramics, and raw rug fibers.

Among the companies owned by the Foundation is ZamZam, Iran's very own revolutionary version of Coca-Cola. ZamZam produces 800 million liters of soft drinks every year and holds approximately 40 percent of the domestic market. Also in the food and beverage industry, the Foundation owns almost 63 percent of the Behnoosh Iran Company, the producer of the non-alcoholic fruit flavored Delster beer and its bottle and can variations. In addition to ZamZam and Behnoosh, the Foundation also controls three other important players in Iran's food industry: Glucozan (glucose, starch of maize, vegetable oil), Ghooshtiran (meat), and a 33 percent stake of Pakdairy (dairy products).

The Foundation has a huge stake in agriculture as well. Its Agricultural Branch controls twelve companies. It owns lands for feed and forage production, and grows various crops (including pistachios). The Animal Husbandry Branch runs 22 farms under the supervision of 17 companies involved in dairy farming, breeding, egg production, animal feed production, poultry, and slaughtering. According to the Foundation's website, its economic interests also include a shipping line through its marine group, the Bonyad Trade & Transport Organization (BTTO). BTTO controls the Bonyad Shipping Company (BOSCO), a Persian Gulf shipping line that owns nine ships, with a controlling position in Bonyad Shipping Agency Co. (BOSACO), Queshm management shipping Co. (QUESHM BONYAD), and Bonyad Stevedoring Co. (BOBACO).

The CEO of *Ghorb*, Abolqasem Mozaffari Shams, is an IRGC officer. Prior to this appointment, he served as the head of the Iran Water and Power Resources Development Company (IWPCo) and as head of the Iran Tunnel Association (IRTA). His previous involvement in these important public-owned institutions further illustrates the level of IRGC penetration of the Iranian state.

According to Alfoneh, *Ghorb* is directed by a council chaired by the IRGC commander-in-chief, General Ali Jafari, and includes the chief of Iran's Joint Forces Command, Brigadier General Mohammed Hejazi; the chiefs of the five separate IRGC forces; Army Chief Brigadier General Mohammad Pakpour; Rear Admiral Navy Chief Ali Fadavi; Brigadier General Hossein Salami of the Air Force; Brigadier General Qasem Soleimani of the Qods Forces; Brigadier General Mohammad Reza Naqdi of the Basij; Brigadier General Dr. Seyyed Ali Hosseini Tash, the head of Imam Hossein University (an IRGC institution of higher education that plays a central role in the nuclear program);[7] the commander of the IRGC Cooperative Foundation;[8] and the head of the IRGC Self Sufficiency Directorate, a branch of the IRGC which promotes economic self-reliance–the Iranian equivalent of Fascism's autarchy and North Korean Juche.

*Ghorb* is one of the most powerful enterprises in Iran. It employs approximately 25,000 people, of whom an estimated 10 percent are IRGC conscripts.[9] Its many companies are involved in hundreds of projects. Since 1988, through *Ghorb*, the IRGC has built dams, highways, water tunnels, ports, bridges, metro systems, public buildings, pipelines, and other important infrastructure.

Abolqasem Mozaffari Shams' predecessor, General Rostam Qasemi, also an IRGC high ranking officer, left the post to become the new oil minister on August 3, 2011.[10] The appointment of one of the most influential IRGC officers to the Oil Ministry marks an additional step in the IRGC takeover of the oil sector, the Iranian economy's most lucrative and most strategic asset. In his capacity as minister of oil, Qasemi will also serve as the head of the Organization of Petroleum Exporting Countries (OPEC) while Iran holds the rotating presidency. Having a U.S.- and EU-sanctioned individual as the head of this powerful oil cartel diminishes the impact of these sanctions.

---

7    Seyyed Ali Hosseini Tash was also Ali Larijani's deputy at the Supreme Council for National Security and as such he was the deputy nuclear negotiator. He was appointed to Imam Hossein University in 2007.

8    A Foundation established to offer preferential financial services to IRGC members.

9    Wherley et al., p. 60: "IRGC commander Sattar Vafaei stated in an interview that about 25,000 engineers and staff work for Khatam al-Anbia. Ten percent of these personnel are IRGC members and the rest are contractors." See also p. 63: "[KAA deputy director, Abdolreza] Abedzadeh emphasized that the IRGC's military activities and Khatam's construction activities are kept "completely separate" and that only 10 percent of Khatam'slabor is derived from IRGC ranks, and the rest consists of subcontractors."

10    Robin Pomeroy & Ramin Mostafavi, "Iran Parliament Makes Military Man Oil Minister," *Reuters*, August 3, 2011, www.reuters.com/article/2011/08/03/us-iran-oil-minister-vote-idUSTRE7722OP20110803.

Furthermore, because European countries often apply and receive exemptions for the travel of high-level officials, EU countries may not have the political will to enforce their own travel bans against Qasemi or any other designated individual who is appointed to a high-level government position. Qasemi is now the fourth sanctioned Iranian individual to receive a new Iranian government title and thereby evade international sanctions. On previous occasions, the European Union dropped or did not enforce travel bans against Iranian Foreign Minister Ali Akbar Salehi, who used to chair the Atomic Energy Organization of Iran and in such a position was in charge of Iran's nuclear program; and Salehi's successor at the AEOI, Fereydoun Abbasi-Davani, a nuclear scientist with IRGC links, previously involved in Iran's clandestine military program, who survived an assassination attempt on November 29, 2010. Iranian Defense Minister Ahmad Vahidi has also been able to travel abroad despite an Interpol red notice for his role in the 1994 AMIA bombing in Argentina.

In the energy sector, the IRGC maintains a loose but fruitful cooperation with the National Iranian Oil Company (NIOC), which controls all Iranian energy interests. According to Fareed Mohamedi and Raad al Kadiri, both partners at the energy consultancy firm PFC Energy:

> Under President Ahmadinejad, the IRGC's influence has grown not only within NIOC, but also in the service sector. Khatam al-Anbia, the construction arm of the IRGC, has strengthened its role throughout the Iranian economy, including the oil and gas sector. In 2006, it won a contract to develop South Pars Phases 15-16. And in 2009, it took over the Sadra yard—a firm that has built many platforms used in the Persian Gulf and the recently completed Alborz semi-submersible rig, which will drill in the Caspian Sea. While this exemplifies the growing strength of the IRGC, it also has led to financing difficulties, as sanctions have deterred banks from funding Phases 15-16 due to its link with Khatam al-Anbia.[11]

The IRGC's involvement in Iran's energy business is significant and growing:

> Khatam al-Anbia is highly active in the oil sector and is said to be operating as the sole contractor for Iran's gas industry. The agency's deputy director for reconstruction, IRGC Brigadier Abdolreza Abedzadeh, said that the

---

11 Fareed Mohamedi & Raad Alkadiri, "Iran: U.S. Sanctions, Iranian Responses and Implications for Investment," A Special Presentation for Petrofed, June 14, 2010, http://petrofed.winwinhosting.net/upload/14june10/summary.pdf.

EMANUELE OTTOLENGHI

company had 247 on-going "industrial and mining" projects and had completed 1,220 projects since 1990. Iran's oil ministry has signed a number of no-bid contracts with the company worth billions of dollars. Government officials claim that these contracts were awarded because of the lower cost offered by the IRGC, its skilled corps of engineers, its experience with large projects, and its access to heavy machinery and sizable assets.[12]

*Khatam al-Anbiya* has also secured contracts for pipelines, including the 560-mile long natural gas pipeline from Bushehr to Sistan-Balochistan, a project worth $1.3 billion according to published estimates by *The Guardian*. It reportedly also has taken over most development phases in the South Pars offshore gas field, partially as a response to foreign companies' withdrawals in the wake of international sanctions.[13]

Naturally, given its origins and history as a reconstruction tool for the Revolution, *Ghorb* was initially involved in infrastructure projects, and it remains heavily invested in that area through its subsidiaries. Its companies have been awarded contracts for the Jaghin, Kharkeh, and Saveh Dams; a metro line in Tehran; a railway between Tabriz and Tehran; hydroelectric and dam constructions projects across the country, such as the Rudbar-e-Lorestan project; water systems like the Dez-Ghomroud river basin system in Khuzestan and the port of Chabahar in Sistan-e Balochistan; and the development of parts of Iran's energy industry, including building basic infrastructure such as jetties and offshore platforms.[14] In addition, through the Basij, the IRGC has carried out an impressive number of small local projects in rural and provincial areas of Iran over the years, including roads, water reservoirs, school buildings and recreational facilities, which are meant to strengthen popular support for the Revolution through local attention to basic social needs.

Most of these projects are straightforward business ventures—although some, like the Chabahar Port, which is currently being expanded to host Russian-made Kilo-class submarines, have military dimensions as well. Regardless, the IRGC's involvement in these activities produces vast profits for the organization, which it uses for military procurement and proliferation purposes.

---

12   Wherley et al., pp. 61-62.

13   Julian Borger & Robert Tait, "The Financial Power of the Revolutionary Guards," *The Guardian*, February 15, 2010, www.guardian.co.uk/world/2010/feb/15/financial-power-revolutionary-guard.

14   See, for example, Sepasad's list of projects at:www.sepasad.com/en/index.php?option=com_phocagallery&view=c ategories&Itemid=50 (accessed May 12, 2011).

The IRGC's legitimate business dealings also enable it to gain access to foreign technology that Iran cannot yet produce indigenously. The IRGC can thus acquire missing tools to advance its military projects, learn critical skills, crack technological secrets, and insofar as it succeeds in reverse-engineering foreign technologies, make Iranian military industries less dependent on imports over time.

It is difficult to measure and name every single endeavor of IRGC business affiliates. But, as Alfoneh writes:

> While mapping such enterprises is difficult, given the opacity of the Iranian economy in general and the IRGC in particular, official and commercial Iranian reporting provides enough data to show just how intertwined the IRGC has become with the economy of the Islamic Republic.[15]

However, before further discussing the IRGC's involvement in Iran's economy and how to identify its companies, a word must be spent on the IRGC's defense capabilities, given that much of its revenues go to fund military procurement, including the country's ballistic missile and nuclear programs.

---

15    Alfoneh, "How Intertwined Are the Revolutionary Guards in Iran's Economy?"

# CHAPTER 6: THE GUARDS IN IRAN'S NATIONAL DEFENSE

The most obvious area of IRGC presence, given the interplay of political influence, economic clout, and military power, is national defense. Iran's Defense Industry Organization (DIOMIL), with its 20,000-strong workforce,[1] is the production and supply instrument of the Islamic Republic's armed forces.

Wholly controlled by the Guards, the Defense Industry Organization has six subsidiaries: Armament Industries; Ammunition and Metallurgy Industries; Chemical Industries and Development of Material; Marine Industries; Special Industries; and Vehicle and Equipment Industries. These organizations produce a wide range of armaments, from bullets and light arms to fast boats, tanks, anti-aircraft systems, and artillery pieces. Indeed, DIOMIL plays an extremely important role in the nation's defense.

As a result of the U.S. military embargo, which took a heavy toll on the Islamic Republic, Iran has made self-sufficiency in producing and procuring critical arms a central tenet of its defense doctrine. With its overseas operations and vast network of front companies abroad, the IRGC has used emissaries, intermediaries, and deception to acquire a number of sophisticated and otherwise inaccessible military items, which it has subsequently copied through reverse engineering and then mass-produced.

Three examples illustrate the IRGC's success in this respect, shedding light on the importance of the interplay among the military, political, and economic spheres of IRGC's influence.

The first involves the sale to Iran of an Italian speedboat by Italian company FB Design, designer and producer of the award-winning racing boat, the *Levriero*. Having obtained an original version of the *Levriero* speedboat, the IRGC reverse-engineered it and began producing an Iranian version. In October 2007, an investigative report by Gianluca Di Feo and Stefania Maurizi for the Italian weekly *L'Espresso* indicated

---

1    The figure provided by the DIOMIL website: www.diomil.ir/en/aboutus.aspx.

that in 1998, Iranian emissaries bought "designs, prototypes, materials and whatever is necessary to produce" the boat.[2] While the Iranian buyer of the speedboats may have appeared to be a businessman seeking the vessels for civilian purposes, he was, in all likelihood, an agent of the IRGC who procured the vessels for its military-industrial complex. Unknown to the Italian firm, the boats were thus acquired through an IRGC front company and, although they were sold for civilian use, quickly modified and assigned a military role.

The London-based *Daily Mail* initially reported the sale of the Italian speedboats in May 2007, following the capture of 15 British sailors by Iranian speedboats on the Shatt al'Arab waterway, which divides Iran and Iraq. British officials were understandably puzzled that the Iranian speedboats could be so fast. The long investigative piece in *L'Espresso* partially answered this question. According to the *Daily Mail*, FB Design sold 20 boats to Iran;[3] *L'Espresso* puts the number at 12. On October 19, 2007, Fabio Buzzi, the founder and owner of the Italian company, told the local paper *La Provincia di Lecco* that he had sold only one vessel before the Italian government revoked the company's export license and suspended further deliveries. There was nothing illegal about this, because, as Buzzi noted, he had sold "boats, not weapons" with a regular export license.[4] But it was too late; the IRGC, not overly concerned about respecting licenses, proceeded to copy the Italian-made design marvel and mass-produce it for its maritime forces.

Indeed, since the late stages of the Iran-Iraq War, when the IRGC tried to disrupt commercial shipping in the Persian Gulf, the Guards have turned their speedboat fleet into a centerpiece of their military strategy in the narrow sea lanes of the crowded Strait of Hormuz. In the event of war, these small boats not only could become deadly weapons but could block commercial traffic in one of the world's most vital waterways. In a conventional confrontation, the U.S. Navy would clearly not view its Iranian adversary as a great threat. Therefore for the past two decades, Iran has pursued a defense doctrine intended to avoid a conventional conflict with formidable enemies.

As Robert Baer astutely notes, "In the Iran-Iraq War, Iran recognized that it won more engagements through unconventional tactics and asymmetrical warfare than

---

2    Stefania Maurizi & Gianluca Di Feo, "Cosí l'Italia Arma Teheran,"*L'Espresso*, October 25, 2007, www.stefaniamaurizi.it/Inchieste/cosi_l_italia_arma_teheran.html.

3    "Miles Tops Charts in Rock and Roll Band," *The Daily Mail*, May 26, 2007, www.dailymail.co.uk/sport/othersports/article-457785/Miles-tops-charts-rock-roll-band.html.

4    Marco Corti, "Produco Superbarche, Non Armi per Gli Ayatollah," Interview with Fabio Buzzi, *La Provincia di Lecco*, October 19, 2007.

it did through mass, frontal assaults. But more important, the Lebanon War, waged in the same time frame, had emerged as a paradigm." According to Baer, Iran drew three lessons from the Lebanon Civil War: one, that "small is better"; second, that a stronger adversary can be beaten in "a war of attrition"; and third that "increasing the size of its army wouldn't necessarily give it an advantage." Iran, therefore, "spent the nineties quietly buying advanced weapons from Russia and China—weapons that would level the playing field but not bankrupt Iran."[5]

U.S. forces have taken note of this threat and recognize its seriousness, particularly after an early January 2008 incident in the Strait of Hormuz, when five Iranian speedboats swarmed a three-ship U.S. Navy convoy. Soon after the incident, *The New York Times* revealed that a 2002 naval war game had anticipated a possible confrontation between the U.S. Navy and the IRGC speedboat fleet. The outcome was staggering:

> In that war game, the Blue Team navy, representing the United States, lost 16 major warships—an aircraft carrier, cruisers and amphibious vessels—when they were sunk to the bottom of the Persian Gulf in an attack that included swarming tactics by enemy speedboats...If the attacks of Sept. 11, 2001, proved to the public how terrorists could transform hijacked airliners into hostage-filled cruise missiles, then the "Millennium Challenge 2002" war game...was a warning to the armed services as to how an adversary could apply similar, asymmetrical thinking to conflict at sea.[6]

Since then, under the leadership of their former and current commanders, Yahya Rahim Safavi and Ali Jafari, the Guards have sought to increase the speed and versatility of their speedboats in preparation for a possible showdown against the U.S. in the Persian Gulf. By wreaking havoc to commercial shipping lanes and inflicting serious damage to their number one enemy, Iran can blunt U.S. forces in the region.[7]

In pursuit of this goal, the IRGC recently laid its hands on another pearl of the speedboat racing world, the Bradstone Challenger, which holds the record for fastest

---

5    Baer, pp. 98-101.

6    Tom Shanker, "Iran Encounter Grimly Echoes '02 War Game," *The New York Times*, January 12, 2008, www.nytimes.com/2008/01/12/washington/12navy.html.

7    See IRGC Navy Commander, Admiral Ali Fadavi's comments: "Iran is capable of closing the Strait of Hormuz at any time, and if the enemy makes the slightest threatening movement to undermine the security of the region, it will receive a very firm response." "Iran Will Close the Strait of Hormuz if Attacked," *Mehr News*, February 7, 2011, www.mehrnews.com/en/newsdetail.aspx?NewsID=1248315.

circumnavigation of the British Isles. The Guards' first attempt to acquire the boat failed, but they eventually succeeded by relying on several intermediaries that carried the boat from Great Britain to South Africa, where it was then transferred onto a Hong Kong-flagged Iranian merchant ship, the MV Diplomat, belonging to The Islamic Republic of Iran Shipping Lines (IRISL).[8] The Diplomat had just been renamed a few months before from its original name, *Iran Mutafeh*, and reflagged in Hong Kong as *The Starry Shine* by an IRISL front company.[9] A last-minute attempt by the U.S. Department of Commerce's Bureau of Industrial Security to block the shipment failed, apparently because its notification to South African authorities, sent by fax over the weekend, was seen too late.[10]

By the time the ship set sail to Iran from South Africa in late January 2009, the boat had been handled by companies and intermediaries in three countries, including in South Africa by a former apartheid-era military officer.[11] Soon after, the IRGC boasted that it had snatched the boat. During a ceremony for the delivery of 12 Zolfaqhar Class speedboats to its fleet, IRGC Navy commander Rear Admiral Ali Fadavi announced that Iran had obtained the Bradstone Challenger and was quoted in the Iranian press as saying: "We acquired the boat from the British and what worries the Americans is that we have equipped it with military gear...By 1390 [the Iranian calendar year for 2011] it will be mass produced and delivered to the IRGC Naval Forces."[12]

This is what seems to have been the fate, as well, of an Austrian high-precision sniper rifle produced by Steyr-Mannlicher. Austria sold Iran 800 HS50 12.7mm

---

8   Details of the case are available at: www.bis.doc.gov/news/2009/tdo_01232009.pdf

9   Gcina Ntsaluba & Stefaans Brümmer, "How SA Company Oiled Iran's War Machine," *Mail & Guardian Online*, September 24, 2010, www.mg.co.za/article/2010-09-24-how-sa-company-oiled-irans-war-machine

10   Guy Dinmore, "UK Speedboat Floats into Iran's Arms," *The Financial Times*, April 4, 2010, www.ft.com/cms/ s/0/2be3b9c2-4021-11df-8d23-00144feabdc0.html#axzz1EDtMib4k. "As the Financial Times has learned from defence and industry sources, Iran did not give up. After the boat passed through at least two more parties, the U.S. got wind in January 2009 it was about to be transferred in the South African port of Durban on to a Hong Kong-flagged Iranian merchant vessel, the Diplomat, bound for the Gulf. The U.S. commerce department's Bureau of Industry and Security asked South African authorities to block the transfer. It voiced concern that Iran's Revolutionary Guards intended to use the boat as a 'fast attack craft.' The bureau noted that similar vessels had been armed with "torpedoes, rocket launchers and anti-ship missiles" with the aim of "exploiting enemy vulnerabilities through the use of 'swarming' tactics by small boats." The loading went ahead because, said one source, no one saw the U.S. notice sent by fax over a weekend. U.S. Special Forces were ready to intercept the Iranian merchant vessel but the operation was called off, the source said.

11   Ntsaluba & Brümmer, "How SA Company Oiled Iran's War Machine." According to the authors of the *Mail & Guardian*'s investigative report, "Willem 'Ters' Ehlers, a former navy officer and Botha's private secretary, is no stranger to apartheid-era embargo-busting. Now his company has shipped the speedboat to Iran, where the elite Revolutionary Guard is mass-producing it as an attack craft armed with torpedoes and missiles."

12   "Torpedo Launcher Boats Join IRGC Fleet," *IslamiDavet*, August 10, 2010, www.islamidavet.com/ english/2010/08/10/torpedo-launcher-boats-join-irgc-fleet/.

(.50 caliber) Steyr-Mannlicher sniper rifles to help Iran's drug-fighting police units combat smugglers from Pakistan and Afghanistan.[13] When the U.S. sanctioned Steyr-Mannlicher, the Austrian Defense Ministry defended the licensed sale as "unimpeachable."[14]

That was in December 2005. By February 2007, U.S. troops had seized more than one hundred such rifles during raids against insurgents in Iraq.[15] Steyr-Mannlicher denied the guns came from the stock it sold Iran. The ones sold to Iran's police all bore license numbers, after all, and were accompanied by end-user certificates.

Given its high precision, this rifle does not lend itself to tampering. The simple act of scraping license numbers would deprive the weapon of a critical few milligrams of weight, thus altering its balance and affecting its performance. If American officials were sure of the origins of such guns, they should have been able to produce some evidence, either of the license numbers or of attempts to tamper with the numbers on the guns themselves, the company maintained. Eventually, the trail went cold and American sources were quoted as backtracking on the story.[16] But soon after Iran's purchase, an exact copy of the HS50, produced by Iran's defense industries, emerged at an arms fair in Iran.

Other reports have suggested that China's South Defense Industries replicated the weapon. Their AMR-2 12.7mm looks suspiciously like a replica of the Austrian rifle that was sold to Iran.[17] Whatever the licensing issue, it is plausible that Iran, having acquired a high-precision weapon from Austria, proceeded to ensure it could be replicated in large quantities to suit its needs, including the supply to Iraqi insurgents of the replica, which could be used to kill U.S. troops in Iraq. A

---

13  Iran is confronting a massive and growing addiction problem among its population. According to the 2010 UN Drug World Report, 42 percent of world opium not converted into heroin is used in Iran (Iran consumes approximately 450 tons of opium); of the opium that is converted to heroin for world markets, 35 tons cross into Iran annually, about half of which are in transit for the European market and the rest is destined for local consumption—making up 5 percent of world consumption. Iran has almost 400,000 heroin users and more than 500,000 opium users according to official statistics. A reliable estimate from 1999 suggested that 2.8 percent of Iran's population aged 15-64 regularly used opiates while 4.2 percent made regular use of cannabis. See United Nations Office on Drug and Crime, *World Drug Report 2010*, www.unodc.org/documents/wdr/WDR_2010/World_Drug_Report_2010_lo-res.pdf.

14  "Austria: Steyr-Mannlicher Arms Sales to Iran 'Legal'," *Turkish Weekly*, December 29, 2005, www.turkishweekly. net/news/24332/austria-steyr-mannlicher-arms-sale-to-iran-legal-.html.

15  Thomas Harding, "Iraqi Insurgents Using Austrian Rifles from Iran," *The Daily Telegraph*, February 13, 2007.

16  Alexander U. Mathé, "Dochkeine Austro-WaffenimIrak," *Die Wiener Zeitung*, March 30, 2007, translation available on the Steyr-Mannlicher U.S. website at: www.steyrarms.com/news/items/article/us-forces-contradict-newspaper-report-no-austrian-weapons-found-with-terrorists/?tx_ttnews[backPid]=9&cHash=87ced18815.

17  John J. Tkacik Jr., "The Arsenal of the Iraq Insurgency," *The Weekly Standard*, August 13, 2007, Vol. 12, No. 45, www.weeklystandard.com/Content/Public/Articles/000/000/013/956wspet.asp.

Pentagon source eventually confirmed the likelihood that the weapons found in Iraq were an Iranian-made replica of the Austrian rifle.[18]

Finally, a footnote on the drug traffic that these guns were supposed to help fight against: Two cables from the U.S. embassy in Baku, which were made public by Wikileaks in late 2010, revealed a significant increase of processed heroin from Iran-based labs into Azerbaijan, en route to their final destinations in Europe. Under the guidance of IRGC Chief Commander Ali Jafari, the IRGC was responsible for running the refining activities and benefiting from the profits.[19] As the second cable notes:

> According to widespread rumor, many Iranians in Baku are involved full- or part-time in Iranian regime-related profit making, sanctions-busting, money laundering, and similar activities. Activities range from assisting Iranian interests "on the side" of pursuing private activities, to working primarily for Iranian government entities. These Iranians' formal businesses in Azerbaijan include factories, construction companies, trading companies, and shops, some of which may be hollow companies hiding illicit or semi-licit activities. Some are also said to be significant actors in obtaining spare parts and equipment for the Revolutionary Guard, raising revenues and managing money for it and/or regime figures, or managing Iran-origin narcotics trafficking.[20]

To summarize: The guns that were meant to fight the drugs went to the military industries for reverse-engineering; the drugs went to refining labs run by the IRGC before entering the European markets; and the profits enriched the IRGC, while the regime claims to have a drugs problem and constantly seeks international aid to fight it.

The above examples open a window to the world of the IRGC, revealing its multidimensional nature—an elite military force, a business, an organized crime syndicate, and a political actor at home and abroad. However, to finance its activities, the IRGC needs access to the international financial system, and it owns or controls several banks for this purpose. They include, but are not limited to:

---

18  Author's interview with a Pentagon official, February 2008.

19  Wikileaks Cablegate, cable from September 24, 2008, published in the Norwegian daily *Aftenposten*, www. aftenposten.no/spesial/wikileaksdokumenter/article3999428.ece.

20  Wikileaks Cablegate, cable from the U.S. Embassy in Baku, March 6, 2009, http://cablesearch.org/cable/view. php?id=09BAKU175&hl=Singapore.

- Bank Sepah and all its affiliates, holdings, investments, and management companies, including foreign branches in London, Paris, Frankfurt, and Rome. This also includes investment affiliates Omid Investment Management Company (OIM Co) and Bank Sepah Brokerage Company (BSB Co). Together with OIM Co and BSB Co, Sepah Bank also owns 62.46 percent of outstanding shares of the Sepah Investment Company;[21]
- Post Bank, a financial institution created after Bank Sepah was hit by international sanctions, to handle all overseas transactions formerly conducted by Bank Sepah;
- Bank Ansar, a newly established bank that was created by the Ansar Foundation (an IRGC entity);
- Toseye Ta'avon Bank, created in July 2009, an offshoot of the IRGC Cooperative Foundation—an instrument established in 1988 to provide support and funding to IRGC companies in securing lands, legal aid and financing for projects.[22]

Iran's state banks have also been used as conduits for financial transactions related to IRGC activities that include nuclear and ballistic missile proliferation. These banks include Bank Melli, Bank Mellat, Bank Saderat, Bank Tejarat, Refah Bank, the Hamburg-based Iranian-European Commerce Bank, and their many subsidiaries and affiliates.

In addition, the IRGC relies on state-owned companies to do its bidding. The aforementioned IRISL, Iran's most prominent shipping line, has been its preferred method of shipment for nuclear program technology and missile parts; for the delivery of arms to Iran's proxies; and generally speaking, for procurement purposes. The international community caught up with Iran's reliance on IRISL for its illicit procurement activities and slapped sanctions on the state-owned company, which was eventually included in the list of designated Iranian entities targeted by UN Security Council Resolution 1929 (See Appendix 5). But Iran has not relented. Instead, it has sought to cover its tracks and protect IRISL from sanctions and scrutiny, by building an elaborate and labyrinthine system of Chinese boxes, shell and front companies, to gain time and shield its fleet from seizure and inspections.

As FDD's journalist-in-residence, Claudia Rosett notes:

---

21 According to Bank Sepah's Annual Report for 2008-2009, the Bank has 18,598 employees and 1,771 branches in Iran; it holds 7 trillion Iranian Rials in investments—the equivalent of almost 700 million USD. The Report is available at www.banksepah.ir/DesktopModules/Contents/assets/documents/Reports/2008-2009_Annual_Report.pdf.

22 With the exception of Bank Toseye Ta'avon, all other banks have been designated by the Department of Treasury's OFAC.

This shell game began around 2008, when the U.S. imposed sanctions on Iran's state shipping company, the Islamic Republic of Iran Shipping Lines, or IRISL, for its role in provisioning Iran's rogue missile and nuclear programs. The U.S. Treasury also blacklisted a slew of IRISL affiliates and 123 of its ships, including all 19 of these merchant ships now flagged to Hong Kong, making it potentially a crime under U.S. law to do business with them. Treasury also began pressuring players outside U.S. jurisdiction to shun Iran's proliferators, or risk being cut off from commerce with the U.S. [23]

In this, Iran has been creative. Ownership of the fleet's ships was moved to newly established companies. The ships' names were regularly changed. Safe havens like the Isle of Man[24] and Hong Kong were relied upon to generate a thick smoke screen under which IRISL ships could still navigate undetected (See Appendix 6 for a list of designated IRISL ships).

The Guards have also used Iran's energy and heavy industry branch offices abroad— such as Kala Naft,[25] the National Iranian Oil Company's overseas procurement company, and Mobarakeh Steel,[26] Iran's biggest steel conglomerate—as fronts to acquire dual-use

23   Claudia Rosett, "Iran's Hong Kong Shipping Shell Game," *The Wall Street Journal*, August 30, 2011, http://online.wsj.com/article/SB10001424053111904199404576536892392729816.html.

24   See for example Allan Urry, "Why did Iran register ships in the Isle of Man?" BBC File on 4, July 14, 2010, www.bbc.co.uk/news/10604897.

25   Iran Watch Entity Listing, available at www.iranwatch.org/suspect/records/Kala-Naft.html. According to Iran Watch, Kala Naft was "Listed by the Japanese government in 2007 as an entity of concern for biological, chemical, and nuclear weapon proliferation; identified by the British government in February 1998 as having procured goods and/or technology for weapons of mass destruction programs (specifically nuclear), in "addition to doing non-proliferation related business;" attempted to procure bellows seals for the Tehran Oil Refining Company, but the procurement was denied on December 1, 2004, by a member state of the Nuclear Suppliers Group (NSG)…" Kala Naft is the National Iran Oil Company's overseas procurement arm.

26   Iran Watch Entity Listing, available at www.iranwatch.org/suspect/records/mobarakeh-steel-complex.html. According to Iran Watch, Mobarakeh Steel was "Listed by the British government in 2008 as an entity of potential concern for WMD-related procurement, and has had export licenses both granted and denied by that government; intended recipient of an automatic casting machine for special steel, the procurement of which was denied in 2005 by a member state of the Nuclear Suppliers Group (NSG); listed as an entity of concern in an early warning document distributed by the German government to industry in May 2002, but has not been re-listed subsequently; affiliated with the National Iranian Steel Company; affiliated with Iran's Ministry of Industries and Mines; subsidiary of the Iranian Mines and Mining Industries Development and Renovation Organization (IMIDRO); in 2004, Mobarakeh Steel Complex transferred to IMIDRO its 30% holding of Ahwaz Steel Commercial & Technical Service GmbH (a.k.a. Ascotec), a steel company that, on November 17, 2003, was denied United States export privileges for five years and ordered to pay a $50,000 penalty to settle charges of violating the U.S. Export Administration Regulations by causing the exportation of vehicle spare parts, computer components, spare parts for mining machinery, switches, rotary hammers, pneumatic hammers and chisels, and electromotors, from the United States to Iran via Germany without the required authorization from the Office of Foreign Assets Control, U.S. Department of the Treasury; manufacturer of hot- and cold-rolled steel, pickled coils, narrow strip coil, tinplate sheet and coil, galvanized coil, and slab…" Ascotec GmbH was identified by the U.S. Department of Treasury as an entity owned or controlled by the Government of Iran and added to OFAC's Specially Designated Nationals' list (SDN) available at www.treasury.gov/ofac/downloads/t11sdn.pdf.

technologies and forbidden raw materials.

Such covers become critical when it comes to Iran's nuclear program. For example, the Guards use Imam Hossein University to provide academic cover for illegitimate nuclear activities.[27] Imam Hossein, the IRGC military college,[28] is funded jointly by Iran's Ministry of Research and Technology, the Ministry of Defense, and the IRGC.[29] Its scientific endeavors include a nuclear physics program and comprehensive research on laser enrichment.[30] Many of its activities are linked to Iran's WMD program;[31] the Government of Australia designated the university in 2010 for its role in proliferation activities.[32]

The Guards' economic interests also include a number of important manufacturing companies. Iran is the Middle East's largest producer of cars. It is believed that the IRGC owns an important share of the Bahman Group, which produces Mazda cars under license.[33]

An IRGC-dominated consortium won the tender for Iran's second mobile phone network in September 2009.[34] The deal illustrates the collusion between the highest echelons of the regime and the IRGC. The consortium of IRGC companies won the privatization bid when the only other competitor was disqualified under the pretext of security concerns.

---

27  Iran Watch Entity Listing, available at www.iranwatch.org/suspect/records/imam-hussein-university-of-the-revolutionary-guards.html.

28  See Steve Schippert, "Holes and Questions in the IAEA Iran Report," *ThreatsWatch.org*, February 27, 2008, http://threatswatch.org/analysis/2008/02/iaea-schweizer-kase/.

29  Philip Sherwell, "Iran's 'Nuclear' University Conceals Research," *The Daily Telegraph*, April 16, 2006, www.telegraph.co.uk/news/worldnews/middleeast/iran/1515907/Irans-nuclear-university-conceals-research.html.

30  Atomic Energy Organization of Iran's head, Dr Fereydoun Abbasi-Davani—who replaced Ali Akbar Salehi as the head of Iran's nuclear program after surviving an assassination attack in November 2010—was the head of the physics department at Imam Hossein University and, according to sources close to the exiled opposition group Mojaheddin-e-Khalk, in charge of the laser enrichment program at IHU. See "Iran names Attacked Scientist Nuclear Chief: Report," *Reuters*, February 13, 2011, www.reuters.com/article/2011/02/13/us-iran-nuclear-chief-idUSTRE71C16F20110213. Abbasi-Davani was named in a *Newsweek* feature piece on the Covert war against Iran as a long-time member of the IRGC. See Christopher Dickey, R.M. Schneiderman & Babak Dehghanpisheh, "Shadow War," *Newsweek*, December 13, 2010, www.newsweek.com/2010/12/13/the-covert-war-against-iran-s-nuclear-program.html. He was also listed by UN Security Council Resolution 1747, www.iaea.org/newscenter/focus/iaeairan/unsc_res1747-2007.pdf, as a "person involved in nuclear or ballistic missile activities" in March 2007.

31  See Anthony H. Cordesman with Adam C. Seitz, *Iranian Weapons of Mass Destruction: Biological Weapons Program*, CSIS, Draft report, October 28, 2008, http://csis.org/files/media/csis/pubs/081028_iranbw_chapterrev.pdf. Cordesman identifies Imam Hossein as being part of the biological weapons program of the Islamic Republic of Iran.

32  Reserve Bank of Australia's Iran Annex, *Attachment A to Sanctions against Iran, Amendment to the Annex*, www.rba.gov.au/media-releases/2010/mr-10-18-attach-a.html.

33  Wherley et al., p. 100.

34  "Revolutionary Guard Buys Stake in Iran Telecom," *The New York Times Book Blog*, September 28, 2009, http://dealbook.nytimes.com/2009/09/28/revolutionary-guard-buys-stake-in-iran-telecom/.

IRGC companies are also prominent in the services and logistics sectors, where energy consulting companies, shipping, and harbor logistics (such as bunkering services and containers) have also fallen under the purview of the IRGC.

As if all of this were not enough, the IRGC runs additional illicit economic activities through airports and harbors. It maintains an almost complete monopoly over the commercial port of Shahid Rajai and reportedly uses Iran's Payam International Airport near Karaj and Payam Air for the sale of refined petroleum products abroad and the smuggling of goods[35] including cars, electronics, and a wide range of household commodities that are either scarce or costly on the U.S.-embargoed and internationally sanctioned domestic market.[36]

It is difficult to give accurate figures about the value of the smuggling trade, considering that it occurs with a considerable degree of connivance. Even so, available literature agrees that it is a business worth billions of U.S. dollars per year. The aforementioned RAND Corporation report states:

> The abundant availability of banned commodities in Iran, including alcoholic beverages and narcotics, has led to allegations of IRGC involvement in illegal smuggling activities. While there are no independent means of substantiating such allegations, the IRGC is the only organization, it is argued, that could engage in such large-scale trafficking, due to its vast networks and access to countless jetties unsupervised by the government. Facilities such as the Martyr Rajai Port Complex in Hormuzgan province are reportedly used to export state subsidized gasoline outside the country. The IRGC is estimated to yield a 200–300 percent profit on such illegal sales. One Majles member recently stated that IRGC black-market activities might account for $12 billion per year. Another parliamentarian suggested that "invisible jetties... and the invisible hand of the mafia control 68 percent of Iran's entire exports." Others claim that a high volume of contraband goods enter the country via "illegal and unofficial channels, such as invisible jetties supervised by strongmen and men of wealth." There are also claims that the IRGC facilitates the transfer of alcohol, cigarettes, and satellite dishes across portions of the Iran-Iraq border that it controls.[37]

---

35   Alfoneh, "How Intertwined Are Iran's Revolutionary Guards in Iran's Economy?"

36   Babak Dehghanpisheh, "Smugglers for the State," *Newsweek*, July 10, 2010, www.newsweek.com/2010/07/10/smugglers-for-the-state.html.

37   Wherley et al,, pp. 64-65.

Finally, the IRGC has a significant share in Iran's media. As a vast business, military and political conglomerate with ideological objectives, the IRGC promotes its revolutionary message and intimidates its opponents through several media sources:

- Sepah News—the IRGC's official website and news agency;
- Sobh-e-Sadeq—the weekly magazine sponsored by the Supreme Leader;
- IRIB—the Islamic Republic of Iran's Broadcast, headed by former IRGC Brigadier General Ezzatollah Zarghami;[38]
- The websites Horizon and Culture of Self-Sacrifice, which promote IRGC values including martyrdom;
- The Basiji News Agency;
- Fars News Agency; and
- Kayhan—The leading daily in the era of the Shah, which the Revolution seized and transformed into its official mouthpiece after 1979, and which is directed by former IRGC member Hossein Shariatmadari.

The Guards' growing role in Iran's economy has not been without controversy. Voices across the political spectrum have criticized the regime for its increasing centralization of the country's industries. The takeover of Iran's telecommunication company in September 2009 unleashed a storm of opposition from political figures as different in their political outlooks as Green Movement leaders Mousavi and Karroubi, former president Rafsanjani, former IRGC member and Member of the Majles Elyas Naderan, and his colleague, Ali Tavakkoli.[39] In the past, Karroubi has also decried the Guards' network of unlicensed ports along the country's southern shores. This control, which even President Ahmadinejad recently denounced, enables them to run smuggling networks and profit from contraband.

The Guards' combination of military, political, and economic power has practically nullified any effort to liberalize Iran's economy. Leaders framed the supposed privatization as an effort to turn public industries into private ones in order to enhance competition, improve services, reduce costs, and strengthen the economy. In the end, however, the regime sold many state assets to IRGC companies at below market value in no-bid contests, giving the regime even more control of the national economy.

---

38  "IRGC's Dominance Over Iran's Politics and Economy – Part 1," *Iran Focus*, May 11, 2010. www.iranfocus.com/en/index.php?option=com_content&view=article&id=20355:irgcs-dominance-over-irans-politics-and-economy--part-1&catid=32:exclusive-reports&Itemid=32.

39  Mohammed Reza Yazdanpanah, "Former and Current Revolutionary Guard Commanders Clash," *Rooz Online*, July 22, 2010, www.roozonline.com/english/news3/newsitem/article/former-and-current-revolutionary-guards-commanders-clash.html.

The profits the IRGC derives from its business interests fund Iran's military, terrorist proxy groups, and other activities inimical to Western interests. As a result, UN, U.S. and EU restrictions against Iran have singled out the IRGC and its affiliated entities for sanctions. Policymakers should continue to target the Guards' business interests with robust sanctions, blacklisting, and isolation.

When IRGC companies are exposed, it can cut them off from considerable revenues. Such blows not only diminish its ability to fund military projects, but also reduce the entities' political clout in the country. By severing IRGC banks' access to the international financial system, denying the IRGC entities credit, exposing them for their affiliations, and forbidding business interactions with them, the international community can reduce both the IRGC's influence inside Iran and its ability to pursue its goals abroad.

But advocating an expansion of sanctions against IRGC companies is one thing—identifying opportunities is quite another. The remainder of this study will explore the policy dilemmas of sanctioning IRGC companies and explain how to identify them both for the benefit of international businesses seeking to remain in good standing, and as a basis for additional sanctions measures.

On June 9, 2010, UN Security Council Resolution 1929 targeted many Iranian companies for their role in the country's efforts to develop its nuclear and ballistic missile programs. Several of these entities belong to the IRGC, placing them on a small but growing list of companies targeted by previous resolutions. UN Resolutions have also listed a number of prominent commanders and other senior IRGC figures for their involvement in Iran's nuclear program or missile proliferation activities. More recently, the U.S. has designated eight high-ranking Iranian figures, including IRGC commanders, for human rights violations. The European Union has passed its own list of designated Iranian officials with command responsibility in the regime's internal repression.[1]

---

1    http://eurlex.europa.eu/LexUriServ/LexUriServ.do?uri=OJ:L:2011:100:0051:0057:EN:PDF and
http://eurlex.europa.eu/LexUriServ/LexUriServ.do?uri=OJ:C:2011:116:0001:0001:EN:PDF

As noted, the IRGC has grown into an enormous conglomerate over the years. Yet so far, the UN has sanctioned only a handful of its companies.

The United States, hoping to adopt punitive measures against the Iranian regime, designated the IRGC itself in 2007, putting the IRGC's Qods Force on the U.S. terror list (Executive Order 13224);[2] and listing the IRGC as a proliferating entity (Executive Order 13382).[3] Since then, the U.S. Treasury has periodically designated additional IRGC companies, including those now listed by Resolution 1929 (See Appendix 3).

The U.S. is not alone in specifically targeting the IRGC. In 2009, the Dutch Parliament called on the EU to include the IRGC on its terror list because of its support for Hamas and Hezbollah. Yet, so far, designations of previously unidentified IRGC companies are few and far between.

There may be three reasons for this. First, Western diplomats and policymakers are reluctant to target the entire IRGC business conglomerate, given its all-encompassing nature in Iran, and the potential for collateral damage. As a senior EU official put it in a background conversation, "the IRGC does everything, from diapers to missiles. We don't like the missiles, but we don't mind the diapers."[4]

Given that IRGC companies are involved in a wide array of activities that may not necessarily be linked to proliferation or the missile program, as the argument goes, they should not be targeted, lest ordinary Iranians, who may work for or benefit from these companies and their activities, suffer. Second, there is an inherent difficulty in identifying IRGC companies—since their *modus operandi* is opaque and their connections are frequently disguised or concealed to facilitate business activities overseas. And third, the IRGC's constituent parts do not act in unison—especially when it comes to business activities. Present and former Guards have personal rivalries and different political views.

These are no doubt sound objections. The "diapers-versus-missiles" distinction is a by-product of European insistence that sanctions not harm Iran's economy or its people. But Iran's legitimate and illegitimate business endeavors cannot be easily disentangled or separated. The profits from the former are used to finance the latter, as IRGC members have occasionally admitted on the record.[5] Identifying IRGC subsidiaries is difficult, but not impossible—as discussed below.

---

2    www.ustreas.gov/offices/enforcement/ofac/programs/terror/terror.pdf.

3    www.treas.gov/offices/enforcement/ofac/programs/wmd/wmd.pdf.

4    Conversation with the author, April 8, 2010.

5    Wherley et al., pp. 63-64.

Critics of sanctions policy note that former IRGC members have expressed strongly divergent political views in a very public fashion. President Ahmadinejad summarily dismissed Ali Larijani as nuclear negotiator and replaced him with another former Guard, Saeed Jalili. And former IRGC commander Mohsen Rezai ran against Ahmadinejad in the 2009 presidential elections. Such differences may be interpreted as a sign of pluralism within the regime, while some may see them as political openings of sorts. In fact, they are simply a matter of personal and family rivalries, class-based distaste, and tactical differences. On the most vital issues—their loyalty to the Supreme Leader, the nature of the regime, and its nuclear and ballistic missile programs—there is little disagreement.

However, at the same time, service in the IRGC or one of its companies is not an automatic indication that a man has played a role in Iran's illegal activities. After all, *Ghorb* and its affiliate companies can employ IRGC conscripts for army wages as labor manpower for their legitimate contracts. Guards are not always involved in illicit activities. What is guaranteed is that their activities, even when geared toward civilian purposes, add to the power and influence of the Guards. The revenues derived from all their activities funds their military endeavors—including support for terrorist groups abroad and the pursuit of nuclear weapons and ballistic missile technology at home.

There is abundant evidence to show that many IRGC companies are used as conduits for illicit transactions; that their revenue flows into IRGC coffers to finance military projects; and that a place in the companies' board or senior management may result more readily from loyalty to the cause than from professional qualifications. As Matthew Frick put it, "the source of the Pasdaran's political clout can be summed up in one word: *alumni*."[6] The connections the IRGC spawns are often based on informal networks of blood ties and bonds established while in uniform, and maintained, in exchange for economic clout and wealth, once the uniform is retired.

Despite all of this, Resolution 1929 targets only those IRGC companies that are demonstrably involved in Iran's illicit procurement efforts, as well as in the industrial complex responsible for nuclear and missile programs. The EU's decision to adopt autonomous measures against Iran on July 26, 2010 led to additional designations of Iranian companies and individuals, including IRGC entities and IRGC senior commanders, starting with the IRGC Chief Commander Ali Jafari. The Australian, Canadian, Japanese, and South Korean governments adopted similar lists between June and September 2010, but none has so far agreed to designate the IRGC as a whole.

---

6    Frick, p. 125.

Is the preference for designating single entities alone, but not the IRGC as a whole, a better policy option? Does it matter? Given the ubiquitous presence of the IRGC in Iran's economy, exposing as many companies as possible could go a long way toward answering this question, at least in practical terms. The more companies publicly linked to the IRGC, the likelier governments will be to designate them. Meanwhile, exposure will alert the business community of the risks involved in doing business with the Guards, even when transactions appear innocuous.

## CHAPTER 8: DIAPERS AND MISSILES

The IRGC's presence in Iran's economy is ever-expanding. According to a *Time Magazine* report in June 2010, the IRGC's main company, *Ghorb*, owns 812 subsidiaries.[1] *Ghorb*'s tentacle structure of holdings and subsidiaries illustrates the challenge officials confront in seeking to deny the IRGC the ability to profit from business with overseas companies.

Although both the U.S. and the EU have designated *Ghorb*, there is no available public list of all its subsidiaries. Technically, companies doing business in Iran should do their due diligence to determine their partners' affiliations, but this is not so simple. Even the U.S. Treasury, having designated the IRGC as a whole, still adds IRGC entities to its list on a regular basis. The reason: It's not easy to know who is who in Iran's business community. IRGC companies do not come with certificates of origin.

Nevertheless, Western governments have a duty to expose Iranian companies' connections to the IRGC. Even if official government designations do not always follow, exposure can still discourage business ties.

It is important for Western governments to identify IRGC entities operating outside Iran, since they may serve as conduits for illegal procurement. Many IRGC entities have one or more overseas subsidiaries to pursue lucrative contracts and acquire valuable technologies. Identifying them can encourage companies to exercise more restraint when looking to sell sensitive technologies. When such transactions occur within the same jurisdictions or between friendly countries, export controls are often less stringent. That is why the IRGC sets up front companies abroad—to facilitate the acquisition of otherwise hard-to-get technology. Exposing these companies' links to the IRGC can go a long way in reducing their effectiveness.

---

1    Massimo Calabresi, "New Iran Sanctions Target Iran Revolutionary Guards," *Time Magazine*, June 10, 2010, www.time.com/time/world/article/0,8599,1995603,00.html.

One way to identify IRGC involvement is not to look for signs of illegitimate activity, but for potentially undesirable applications of the associated technologies. In 2001, the German company Wirth and the Italian company Seli began work on Iran's Ghomroud water tunnel. The project, in the arid mountains of Khuzestan around the Dez Ghomroud river basin, involved boring four tunnels, divided into several lots. Work began in 2001 and continued for several years.

The contracting company for the project, *Gharargah-e Sazandegi Ghaem*, is, as noted above, none other than *Ghorb*, the construction headquarters of the IRGC. Wirth and Seli supplied equipment in 2003 and 2004. In subsequent years, after becoming aware of the risks associated with working with the IRGC, the companies refrained from delivering further equipment and withdrew from an additional project around the Kerman River, which they had initially agreed to undertake. Eventually, *Ghorb* and several of its subsidiaries were identified and designated, first by the U.S. Treasury and then by the UN, the EU, and other governments.

Though the water tunnel project was entirely civilian in nature, the boring machinery and ventilation equipment, in the hands of the IRGC, were suitable for less innocuous uses. Most Iranian clandestine nuclear sites and ballistic missile silos are reportedly underground, and this technology could clearly be used to dig such facilities. The secret enrichment site near Qom, which was exposed by President Barack Obama, French President Nicholas Sarkozy and then-British prime minister Gordon Brown during the G-20 summit in Pittsburgh in September 2009, is dug deep underground. The technology and expertise Wirth and Seli unwittingly provided to the IRGC are ideal for such projects.

Unless it knows in advance which entities are concealing ulterior motives and likely violating end-user licenses, a company doing business in Iran could end up offering valuable assets to a partner that engages in criminal conduct. Without legislation forbidding deals with the IRGC and its affiliates, companies may turn a blind eye to the identities of their partners. As a result, IRGC companies will continue to acquire advanced technologies and profit from Western countries' insistence that legitimate business by IRGC entities has no impact on proliferation. The Ghomroud project illustrates the difficulty of separating diapers from missiles in Iran and highlights the need for more official designations.

Take, again, the example of Ghomroud. The Iranian company responsible for phase five of the Ghomroud project was Sahel Consulting Engineers. In October 2007, the U.S. Treasury designated Sahel as a subsidiary of the IRGC. According to information published on the Italian firm Seli's website, the client for phases three and four was *Ghaem*, a.k.a., *Ghorb*. The tunnel project was contracted to another Iranian company, Pars Geometry, which claims to be private and independent, but whose board members were almost all associated with Sahel in the past. Its CEO was even employed as an engineer at Iran's Ministry of Jihad during the 1980s.

For companies, digging through the layers of deception that IRGC companies employ to mask their identities can be a nightmare—or a pretext to justify purported ignorance about their partners. But for governments, targeting the IRGC as a whole is less important than identifying and naming its myriad business offspring one by one. The more IRGC companies are exposed, the likelier the chances that they will be designated—if not by the UN, then by the U.S., and hopefully the EU, as well.

One more example may illustrate the importance of exposing Iranian entities whose behavior fails the basic tests of corporate transparency.

Iran's presence in Europe and overseas is characterized by subsidiaries, distributors, agents, joint ventures, and other tools that put several layers between local clients, suppliers in the West, and end users in Iran. One such case is Sazeh Consultants Engineering and Construction, an important Iranian engineering consultancy. Sazeh's English-only website[2] informs visitors that the company maintains overseas offices in Calgary, Canada and the Netherlands.

Sazeh's presence in Calgary would not be unusual. Other Iranian energy companies have offices there, like the National Iranian Oil Company (NIOC)'s procurement arm, Kala Naft, which has engaged in proliferation activities.[3]

But unlike Kala Naft, Sazeh offers no information about its offices or activities in Canada, and it has now removed information about its European operations as well. Older information still available online allows one to take a cursory glance at these companies, revealing a pattern of concealment. Some of the companies are dormant—their papers show that the companies have engaged in no significant commercial activities for the last 10 years. In one case, a Chinese-box pattern of ownership reveals inextricable links between the subsidiary companies, as well as an effort to cover the company's tracks. Iranian nationals holding European nationalities own overseas operations—and open source information reveals administrative links among all the companies, though the link to the mother company in Iran is usually concealed.

---

2    www.sazeh.com

3    Iran Watch Entity Listing, available at www.iranwatch.org/suspect/records/Kala-Naft.html, see also in Chapter 6: The Guards in Iran's National Defense, footnote 26

None of the above, taken alone, amounts to more than circumstantial evidence. But together, they raise many red flags. Much of the information the businesses provide is incomplete, misleading, out of date, or altogether false. Whether or not Sazeh is linked to the IRGC, this Iranian company clearly has something to hide.

A similar story surrounds a petrochemical procurement company based in London— PCCUK Ltd (a.k.a. Petrochemical Commercial Company UK Ltd.). PCCUK is a wholly owned subsidiary of the National Petrochemical Company of Iran, which is a subsidiary of the National Iranian Oil Company and Iran's Ministry of Petroleum. The CEO of the company is Seyyed Mohsen Tasalloti,[4] a former IRGC commander with a successful career in the oil sector. His appointment as minister of oil in 2005 by Ahmadinejad did not make it through the Majles;[5] his consolation prize was the job of CEO at a London-based subsidiary of NPC—an entity of concern for the British government due to suspected proliferation activities.[6] He is still based in London.

These are just some among the many companies that are heavily involved in Iran's energy sector, have overseas business ventures, win lucrative energy contracts with European investment, and benefit from European technological know-how. Their practices reveal a consistent lack of transparency, an influential IRGC presence among its senior management, and a system that obscures the trail of companies that eventually leads back to a single Iranian company.

These companies follow a similar pattern. Beneath a seemingly innocuous surface, one finds an incredible amount of incongruent information. By following each suspicious lead, often one discovers more contradictory details. Some potential IRGC front companies provide names and biographies of their directors and board members, and when they do, it can expose suspicious administrative connections.

Tidewater PLC,[7] a company listed on opposition websites as belonging to the IRGC, and recently designated for its IRGC connections by the U.S. Department of Treasury, presents itself as a shipping company. Its website says nothing of the identity and composition of the board of directors, CEO, or executive officers. It

---

4    See details at www.companiesintheuk.co.uk/ltd/petrochemical-commercial-company-%28uk%29.

5    "Iran's President Names Revolutionary Guards Commander as Oil Chief," *Iran Focus*, November 16, 2005, www.iranfocus.com/en/index.php?option=com_content&view=article&id=4446:irans-president-names-revolutionary-guards-commander-as-oil-chief&catid=3:special-wire.

6    For details, see www.iranwatch.org/suspect/records/national-petrochemical-company.html.

7    www.tidewater.ir/English/EN_Home.aspx

does, however, include a "Martyrs' memorial"[8] for its fallen employees during the Iran-Iraq War (which it refers to as "The Imposed War"). And its history section indicates that the company was managed throughout the 1980s by entities clearly linked to the Islamic revolution, including the two IRGC-controlled revolutionary foundations, the Foundation of the Oppressed and the Martyrs' Foundation of the Islamic Revolution.[9]

Tidewater lists numerous subsidiaries and the curriculum vitae of some of their board members. For example, the board of directors for *Efthekhar Saham*, an investment and import/export company, includes Mohammad Saeed Garoosi, a former adviser for the Sepah Investment Company (a holding company of the IRGC's Bank Sepah) and Mohammad Bidgeli, who also worked as managing director for Sepah Investment and later for Omid Investment Management Company (another holding of Bank Sepah).

In another case, *Rahyab Rayaneh Ghostar*'s vice chairman, Davood Mohammadian, holds a Ph.D. in artificial intelligence and formerly served as an adviser to the minister of defense and the Supreme Leader.[10]

It would be hard to imagine a man more connected with the Iranian regime.

---

8   www.tidewater.ir/English/TidewaterCo/En_history.aspx

9   *Ibid.*

10   www.tidewater.ir/English/Companys/En_Rahyab.aspx.

## CHAPTER 9: IDENTIFYING CRITERIA

With a little effort, governments and corporations can often ascertain the nature of Iranian companies. They can also identify suspicious links and deceptive practices. But companies can only go so far. Governments, with their intelligence capabilities, must go the extra mile to confirm the identity of the IRGC's front companies. Exposing them in great numbers would provide an invaluable public service, especially in Europe, where officials hesitate to move against legitimate businesses. It would also be of great help to the business community in showcasing the systematic misconduct of IRGC businesses. Designating as many of them as possible would also, in practice, reduce the gap between those who wish to target the IRGC as a whole and those who wish to draw the diapers/missiles distinction.

In most cases, IRGC companies cannot remain invisible. Because they seek to engage in business transactions, they need to provide enough information to appear legitimate. In sifting through that information, one often finds a number of common features that should always arouse suspicion:

- Overseas operations lacking transparency;
- Past or ongoing associations with one or more known IRGC entities through shareholders, managers, personnel, or projects;
- Involvement in public contracts linked to the IRGC;
- Extensive operations in diverse areas—covering everything from infrastructure to logistics, services to finance, energy to shipping; and
- Noticeable discrepancies in the information provided by the English and Farsi websites or by the parent companies and the subsidiaries.

Not all Iranian companies serve the IRGC and its purposes. Nor do all Iranian efforts to procure technology abroad fulfill sinister goals. But where they do, U.S. and European policymakers should endeavor to expose the incongruities and reveal IRGC connections. They must continue to inform their friends, allies, and business communities about Iranian companies' ties to the Guards.

To this end, Western governments should designate as many IRGC companies as they can. Ultimately, these are the companies that finance Tehran's illegal nuclear program, train and bankroll terror organizations, and enable the regime to jail, torture and kill its democratic opponents. They should not profit from business relations with the West.

# CHAPTER 10: CONCLUSION

Born as a people's militia in charge of protecting the Revolution, the IRGC has traveled a long way since its early days.

Today, under the leadership of General Ali Jafari, the IRGC holds the key to power because, in the little more than three decades since the Iranian Revolution, it has established itself as an army. It controls the security and intelligence apparatus of the country, operates its own defense industry, runs cutting-edge missile and nuclear programs, penetrates the political system by placing loyalists in key positions of power, and increases its ownership of the economy.

The Guards' strength rests on the fact that, throughout the turmoil of revolution, war, reconstruction, reforms, economic boom, nuclear exposure, sanctions and now the democratic stirrings of a nation tired of both Islam and Revolution, they have remained brothers in arms and ideological devotees to the core principles of the Islamic system of governance created by the late Ayatollah Khomeini under the banner of *velayat-e faqih*.

They are truly devoted to that unique ideological blend that is Khomeini's message—an explosive combination of the subversive with the divine, which makes modern Iran a powerful, if sometimes uneasy blend of revolutionary fervor and Islamic piety.

The powerful combination of Islamic grievance and Persian national pride has not been an easy act to balance. The Governance of the Jurist has not been without controversy—and the difficult task of reconciling the demands of Islamic governance and the imperial ambitions of a rising regional power with a glorious past to reassert and the constraints of state have added strains.

Finally, the rhetoric of injustice and grievance that so powerfully inspired the Shi'a community throughout its history is under unprecedented assault today, as the Revolution that aspired to rise in defense of the oppressed is considered as an oppressor by a vast sector of the very same society it was supposed to deliver from oppression.

The Guards view the tumult as a threat to the system. They are in control of formidable military and financial resources to quell any opposition—and they have the proven ability to use ruthless force to repel any attack. And unless future Iranian history offers surprises similar to the ones that, in the early months of 2011, rocked the Arab world, the IRGC will likely continue to be a significant power in Iran.

There is still much to be written about this elusive player in the opaque and intricate landscape of Iranian politics. Western democracies, for their part, have just begun to take stock of the nature of this threat and have only recently undertaken the first, tentative steps required to meet it. Much more needs to be done to effectively confront the IRGC.

Policymakers must therefore study the IRGC—Iran's veritable power behind the throne—and develop coherent policies to curb its influence, harm its stranglehold on the economy, thwart its networks abroad, and aggressively isolate its leadership and its tentacle-like reach both inside the country and beyond Iran's borders.

This is a daunting task. Yet it is a challenge that cannot be skirted. Today, more than ever, confronting Iran means confronting the IRGC in its multiple and expanding roles as supporter of terrorism, financier of Islamic extremism, enabler of anti-Western coalitions, organized crime ring in charge of smuggling drugs, chief nuclear and ballistic missile proliferator, and the principal destabilizing force in the Middle East.

EMANUELE OTTOLENGHI

# Command Structure of Iran's Islamic Revolutionary Guard Corps

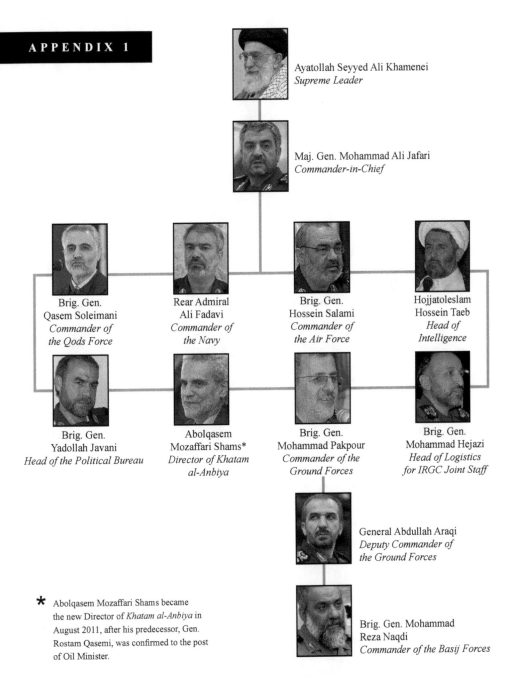

**APPENDIX 1**

Ayatollah Seyyed Ali Khamenei
*Supreme Leader*

Maj. Gen. Mohammad Ali Jafari
*Commander-in-Chief*

Brig. Gen.
Qasem Soleimani
*Commander of
the Qods Force*

Rear Admiral
Ali Fadavi
*Commander of
the Navy*

Brig. Gen.
Hossein Salami
*Commander of
the Air Force*

Hojjatoleslam
Hossein Taeb
*Head of
Intelligence*

Brig. Gen.
Yadollah Javani
*Head of the Political Bureau*

Abolqasem
Mozaffari Shams*
*Director of Khatam
al-Anbiya*

Brig. Gen.
Mohammad Pakpour
*Commander of the
Ground Forces*

Brig. Gen.
Mohammad Hejazi
*Head of Logistics
for IRGC Joint Staff*

General Abdullah Araqi
*Deputy Commander of
the Ground Forces*

**∗** Abolqasem Mozaffari Shams became
the new Director of *Khatam al-Anbiya* in
August 2011, after his predecessor, Gen.
Rostam Qasemi, was confirmed to the post
of Oil Minister.

Brig. Gen. Mohammad
Reza Naqdi
*Commander of the Basij Forces*

# Top Commanders of Iran's Islamic Revolutionary Guard Corps

**Mohammad Ali Jafari is** the Commander of Iran's Islamic Revolutionary Guard Corps (IRGC). Under his command, the IRGC participated in beatings and arbitrary arrests of peaceful protestors after the June 2009 election (Source: U.S. Department of Treasury).

## In Alphabetical Order

**Abdullah Araqi** is the Deputy Commander of the IRGC. Araqi is outspoken on Iran's missile capabilities (Source: Council on Foreign Relations).

**Ali Fadavi** is the Commander of the IRGC Navy. Fadavi often speaks about Iran's ability to project power in the Strait of Hormuz through its increased naval capabilities (Source: Islami Davet).

**Mohammed Hejazi** is the head of Logistics for the IRGC Joint Staff. Prior to that, he was Commander of the Basij Forces (Source: U.S. Department of Treasury).

**Yadollah Javani** is the head of the IRGC Political Bureau. Javani makes frequent statements about Iran's missile program (Source: Iran Focus).

**Abolqasem Mozaffari Shams** became Director of *Khatam al-Anbiya* in August 2011. His predecessor, Rostam Qasemi was designated by the U.S. and the EU for proliferation activities. As of August 2011, Mozaffari Shams has not been similarly designated (Source: Fars News Agency).

**Mohammad Reza Naqdi** is the Commander of the IRGC's Basij Forces. Naqdi was linked to recent Basij abuses, including the violent response to the December 2009 Ashura Day protests (Source: U.S. Department of Treasury).

**Mohammad Pakpour** is the Commander of the IRGC Army. Previously, he was the senior commander of IRGC forces inside Lebanon and was responsible for Iranian financial support to Hezbollah
(Source: Stratfor).

**Rostam Qasemi** was confirmed as the Minister of Oil on August 3, 2011. He had been Director of *Khatam al-Anbiya*. He holds the rank of General in the IRGC
(Source: Associated Press).

**Hossein Salami** is the Commander of the IRGC Air Force. Salami has made frequent comments about Iran's missile capabilities (Source: *The Globe and Mail).*

**Qasem Soleimani** is the Commander of the IRGC's Qods Force, a special unit in charge of exporting Iran's Islamic Revolution (Source: U.S. Department of Treasury).

**Hossein Taeb** is the head of Intelligence for the IRGC. Previously, he was the head of the Basij Forces (Source: U.S. Department of Treasury).

# Designation of IRGC Companies By the U.S., EU, UN and Other Western Allies

| IRGC Company | Authority & Legislation | Designation Date | Reason for Designation |
|---|---|---|---|
| Iran Air | U.S. Treasury, Executive Order 13382 | June 23, 2011 | Providing material support and services to the IRGC |
| Ansar Bank | U.S. Treasury, Executive Order 13382 | December 21, 2010 | Providing financial services to the IRGC |
| | EU Commission Regulation No. 503/2011 | May 23, 2011 | Involvement in Iran's nuclear or ballistic weapons activities; Created to provided financial and credit services to the IRGC |
| Basij Force | U.S. Treasury, Executive Order 13553 | June 9, 2011 | Controlled by the IRGC |
| Bank Melli | U.S. Treasury, Executive Order 13382 | October 25, 2007 | Providing banking services to the IRGC and Qods Force |
| Bonyad Taavon Sepah | U.S. Treasury, Executive Order 13382 | December 21, 2010 | Providing services to the IRGC |
| | EU Commission Regulation No. 503/2011 | May 23, 2011 | Controlled by the IRGC; Designated for its involvement in Iran's nuclear or ballistic missile activities |

| IRGC Company | Authority & Legislation | Designation Date | Reason for Designation |
|---|---|---|---|
| Fater (or Faater) Institute | U.S. Treasury, Executive Order 13382 | February 10, 2010 | Owned or controlled by Khatam al-Anbiya |
| | UNSC Resolution 1929 | June 9, 2010 | Owned or controlled by, or acting on behalf of, the Islamic Revolutionary Guard Corps |
| | EU Commision Regulation No. 532/2010 | June 18, 2010 | Subsidiary of Khatam al-Anbiya; owned or controlled by, or acting on behalf of the IRGC |
| Gharagahe Sazandegi Ghaem | U.S. Treasury, Executive Order 13382 | October 25, 2007 | Owned or controlled by the IRGC |
| | UNSC Resolution 1929 | June 9, 2010 | Owned or controlled by Khatam al-Anbiya |
| Ghorb Nooh | U.S. Treasury, Executive Order 13382 | October 25, 2007 | Owned or controlled by the IRGC |
| | UNSC Resolution 1929 | June 9, 2010 | Owned or controlled by Khatam al-Anbiya |
| | EU Commision Regulation No. 532/2010 | June 18, 2010 | Owned or controlled by the IRGC and Khatam al-Anbiya |
| Ghorb-e Karbala | U.S. Treasury, Executive Order 13382 | October 25, 2007 | Owned or controlled by the IRGC |
| | UNSC Resolution 1929 | June 9, 2010 | Owned or controlled by Khatam al-Anbiya |
| | EU Commision Regulation No. 532/2010 | June 18, 2010 | Owned or controlled by the IRGC and Khatam al-Anbiya |
| Hara Company | U.S. Treasury, Executive Order 13382 | October 25, 2007 | Owned or controlled by the IRGC |
| | UNSC Resolution 1929 | June 9, 2010 | Owned or controlled by Ghorb Nooh |
| | EU Commision Regulation No. 532/2010 | June 18, 2010 | Owned or controlled by the IRGC and Ghorb Nooh |
| Imam Hossein University | Australia: Charter of the United Nations (Santions-Iran) (Specified Entities) List 2010 | July 29, 2010 | Designated as an entity of the IRGC |

| IRGC Company | Authority & Legislation | Designation Date | Reason for Designation |
|---|---|---|---|
| Imensazan Consultant Engineers Institute | U.S. Treasury, Executive Order 13382 | February 10, 2010 | Owned or controlled by Khatam al-Anbiya |
| | UNSC Resolution 1929 | June 9, 2010 | Owned or controlled by Khatam al-Anbiya |
| | EU Commision Regulation No. 532/2010 | June 18, 2010 | Owned or controlled by the IRGC and Khatam al-Anbiya |
| Iran Marine Industrial Company (SADRA) | EU Commission Regulation No. 503/2011 | May 23, 2011 | Owned or controlled by Khatam al-Anbiya |
| IRGC Air Force | Council of the European Union | June 23, 2008 | Operates Iran's inventory of short and medium range ballistic missiles |
| IRGC Air Force Al-Ghadir Missile Command | Council of the European Union, No. 668/2010 | July 26, 2010 | Has operational control of Iran's missiles |
| IRGC-Qods Force (IRGC-QF) | U.S. Treasury, Executive Order 13224 | October 25, 2007 | Provides military support to numerous terrorist groups including the Taliban |
| | Council of the European Union, No. 668/2010 | July 26, 2010 | Responsible for IRGC operations outside of Iran |
| Khatam al-Anbiya Construction Headquarters | U.S. Treasury, Executive Order 13382 | October 25, 2007 | Owned or controlled by the IRGC |
| | UNSC Resolution 1929 | June 9, 2010 | Owned by the IRGC |
| | EU Commision Regulation No. 532/2010 | June 18, 2010 | Owned by the IRGC |
| Liner Transport Kish (LTK) | U.S. Treasury, Executive Order 13382 | December 21, 2010 | The IRGC has used the company to support terrorist activities outside of Iran. |
| Makin | U.S. Treasury, Executive Order 13382 | February 10, 2010 | Owned or controlled by Khatam al-Anbiya |
| | UNSC Resolution 1929 | June 9, 2010 | Owned or controlled by Khatam al-Anbiya |
| | EU Commision Regulation No. 532/2010 | June 18, 2010 | Owned or controlled by the IRGC and Khatam al-Anbiya |

| IRGC Company | Authority & Legislation | Designation Date | Reason for Designation |
|---|---|---|---|
| Mehr Bank | U.S. Treasury, Executive Order 13382 | December 21, 2010 | Providing financial services to the IRGC |
| | EU Commission Regulation No. 503/2011 | May 23, 2011 | Controlled by Bonyas Taavon and the IRGC; provides financial services to the IRGC |
| Mehr Eghtesad Iranian Investment Company | U.S. Treasury, Executive Order 13382 | June 23, 2011 | Owned or controlled by Mehr Bank |
| Naserin Vahid | Council of the European Union, No. 668/2010 | July 26, 2010 | An IRGC front company that produces weapons parts on behalf of the IRGC |
| | Australia: Charter of the United Nations (Santions-Iran) (Specified Entities) List 2010 | July 29, 2010 | Designated as an entity of the IRGC |
| Omran Sahel | U.S. Treasury, Executive Order 13382 | October 25, 2007 | Owned or controlled by the IRGC |
| | UNSC Resolution 1929 | June 9, 2010 | Owned or controlled by Ghorb Nooh |
| Oriental Oil Kish | U.S. Treasury, Executive Order 13382 | October 25, 2007 | Owned or controlled by the IRGC |
| | UNSC Resolution 1929 | June 9, 2010 | Owned or controlled by Khatam al-Anbiya |
| Pars Aviation Services Company | UNSC Resolution 1747 | March 24, 2007 | Identified as an entity of the IRGC that maintains various aircraft used by IRGC Air Force |
| Qods Aeronautics Industries | UNSC Resolution 1747 | March 24, 2007 | IRGC has boasted of using this company's products as part of its asymmetric warfare doctrine. |
| Rah Sahel | UNSC Resolution 1929 | September 6, 2010 | Owned or controlled by Khatam al-Anbiya |
| | EU Commision Regulation No. 532/2010 | June 16, 2010 | Owned or controlled by the IRGC and Khatam al-Anbiya |

| IRGC Company | Authority & Legislation | Designation Date | Reason for Designation |
|---|---|---|---|
| **Rahab Engineering Institute** | U.S. Treasury, Executive Order 13382 | February 10, 2010 | Owned or controlled by Khatam al-Anbiya |
| | UNSC Resolution 1929 | June 9, 2010 | Owned or controlled by Khatam al-Anbiya; subsidiary of Khatam al-Anbiya |
| | EU Commision Regulation No. 532/2010 | June 16, 2010 | Owned or controlled by the IRGC and Khatam al-Anbiya; subsidiary of Khatam al-Anbiya |
| **Sahel Consultant Engineering** | U.S. Treasury, Executive Order 13382 | October 25, 2007 | Owned or controlled by the IRGC |
| | UNSC Resolution 1929 | June 9, 2010 | Owned or controlled by Ghorb Nooh |
| | EU Commision Regulation No. 532/2010 | June 16, 2010 | Owned or controlled by the IRGC and Ghorb Nooh |
| **Sepanir** | UNSC Resolution 1929 | June 9, 2010 | Owned or controlled by Khatam al-Anbiya |
| | EU Commision Regulation No. 532/2010 | June 16, 2010 | Owned or controlled by the IRGC and Khatam al-Anbiya |
| **Sepasad Engineering Company** | U.S. Treasury, Executive Order 13382 | October 25, 2007 | Owned or controlled by the IRGC |
| | UNSC Resolution 1929 | June 9, 2010 | Owned and controlled by Khatam al-Anbiya |
| | EU Commision Regulation No. 532/2010 | June 16, 2010 | Owned or controlled by the IRGC and Khatam al-Anbiya |
| **Sho'a Aviation** | UNSC Resolution 1747 | March 24, 2007 | Identifed as an entity of the IRGC whose products the IRGC uses as part of its asymmetric warfare strategy |
| **Tidewater Company** | U.S. Treasury, Executive Order 13382 | June 23, 2011 | Owned by Mehr-e Eqtesad-e Iranian Investment Company, Mehr Bank and the IRGC |

# Designation Of IRGC-Affiliated Individuals By the U.S., EU, UN And Other Western Allies

| IRGC Affiliated Individuals | Authority & Legislation | Designation Date | Reason for Designation |
|---|---|---|---|
| Vice Admiral Ali Akhbar Ahmadian | U.S. Treasury, Executive Order 13382 | October 25, 2007 | Former Chief of the IRGC Joint Chief of Staff |
| | UNSC Resolution 1747 | March 24, 2007 | Chief of IRGC Joint Staff |
| | EU Commission Regulation No. 441/2007 | April 20, 2007 | Chief of IRGC Joint Staff |
| Hushang Allahdad | U.S. Treasury, Executive Order 13224 | August 3, 2010 | Financial officer of the IRGC-Qods Force |
| Brigadier-General Javad Darvish-Vand | Council Decision of June 23, 2008 Implementing Article 7(2) of Regulation (EC) No. 423/2007 | June 24, 2008 | IRGC Brigadier-General; Minister of Defense and Armed Forces Logistics (MODAFL) Deputy for Inspection; Responsible for all MODAFL facilities and installations |
| Rear Admiral Ali Fadavi | Council of the European Union, No. 668/2010 | July 26, 2010 | Commander of the IRGC Navy |
| Brigadier-General Seyyed Mahdi Farahi | EU Council Decision of June 23, 2008 Implementing Article 7(2) of Regulation (EC) No. 423/2007 | June 24, 2008 | IRGC Brigadier-General; Managing Director of the Defence Industries Organisation (DIO) which is designated under UNSCR 1737 (2006) |
| Parviz Fatah | Council of the European Union, No. 668/2010 | July 26, 2010 | Deputy Commander of Khatam al-Anbiya |
| | U.S. Treasury, Executive Order 13382 | December 21, 2010 | Acting on behalf of and providing services to Bonyad Taavon Sepah which was designated for providing services to the IRGC |

| IRGC Affiliated Individuals | Authority & Legislation | Designation Date | Reason for Designation |
|---|---|---|---|
| Brigadier General Mohammad Hejazi | U.S. Treasury, Executive Order 13382 | October 25, 2007 | Former commander of the Basij designated for his connections to the IRGC |
| | UNSC Resolution 1747 | March 24, 2007 | Commander of the Basij |
| Brigadier General Ali Hoseynitash | EU Council Decision of June 23, 2008 Implementing Article 7(2) of Regulation (EC) No. 423/2007 | June 24, 2008 | Head of the General Department of the Supreme National Security Council involved in formulating policy on the nuclear issue |
| Mohammad Ali Jafari | EU Council Decision of June 23, 2008 Implementing Article 7(2) of Regulation (EC) No. 423/2007 | June 24, 2008 | Commander of the IRGC |
| | U.S. Treasury, Executive Order 13382 | June 16, 2010 | Commander of the IRGC |
| Colonel Hasan Mortezavi | U.S. Treasury, Executive Order 13224 | August 3, 2010 | Senior officer of the Qods Force; provides financial and material support to the Taliban |
| General Hossein Musavi | U.S. Treasury, Executive Order 13224 | August 3, 2010 | Commander of the Qods Force Ansar Corps; provides financial and material support to the Taliban |
| Brigadier General Mostafa Mohammad Najjar | EU Council Decision of June 23, 2008 Implementing Article 7(2) of Regulation (EC) No. 423/2007 | June 24, 2008 | Minister of MODAFL; responsible for all military programs, including ballistic missiles programs |
| Brigadier General Mohammad Reza Naqdi | UNSC Resolution 1803 | March 3, 2008 | Former Deputy Chief of the Armed Forces General Staff for Logistics and Industrial Research/Head of the State Anti-Smuggling Headquarters; engaged in efforts to get around sanctions imposed by UNSC Resolutions 1737 and 1747 |
| | U.S. Treasury, Executive Order 13382 | June 16, 2010 | Head of the IRGC's Basij Force since October 2009 |
| | EU Council Implementing Regulation No. 668/2010 | July 26, 2010 | Commander of the Basij Force |

| IRGC Affiliated Individuals | Authority & Legislation | Designation Date | Reason for Designation |
|---|---|---|---|
| **Brigadier General Mohammad Pakpur** | EU Council Implementing Regulation No. 668/2010 | July 26, 2010 | Commander of IRGC Ground Forces |
| **General Rostam Qasemi (aka Rostam Ghasemi)** | U.S. Treasury, Executive Order 13382 | February 10, 2010 | Commander of Khatam al-Anbiya (IRGC construction arm) |
| | EU Council Implementing Regulation No. 668/2010 | July 26, 2010 | Commander of Khatam al-Anbiya (IRGC construction arm) |
| | Banking (Foreign Exchange) Regulations 1959 Sanctions against Iran – Amendment to the Annex | July 21, 2010 | Commander of Khatam al-Anbiya (IRGC construction arm) |
| **Brigadier General Morteza Rezaie** | UNSC Resolution 1747 | March 24, 2007 | Deputy Commander of the IRGC |
| | EU Commission Regulation No. 441/2007 | April 20, 2007 | Deputy Commander of the IRGC |
| | U.S. Treasury, Executive Order 13382 | October 25, 2007 | Deputy Commander of the IRGC |
| **Rear Admiral Morteza Safari** | UNSC Resolution 1747 | March 24, 2007 | Commander of the IRGC Navy |
| | EU Commission Regulation No. 441/2007 | April 20, 2007 | Commander of the IRGC Navy |
| **Major General Yahya Rahim Safavi** | UNSC Resolution 1737 | December 23, 2006 | Former Commander in Chief of the IRGC; involved in Iran's nuclear and ballistic missile programs |
| | EU Council Common Position 2007/140/CFSP | February 27, 2007 | Commander of the IRGC |
| | U.S. Treasury, Executive Order 13382 | July 8, 2008 | Designated for WMD activities; Safavi was replaced as IRGC Commander and appointed as advisor and senior aide for Armed Forces Affairs to the Supreme Leader of the Islamic Republic of Iran Ayatollah Seyyed Ali Khamenei in September 2007. |

| IRGC Affiliated Individuals | Authority & Legislation | Designation Date | Reason for Designation |
|---|---|---|---|
| **Brigadier General Hossein Salami** | EU Council Implementing Regulation No. 668/2010 | July 26, 2010 | Deputy Commander of the IRGC |
| **General Hosein Salimi** | UNSC Resolution 1737 | December 23, 2006 | Commander of the IRGC Air Force; involved in Iran's ballistic missile program |
| | EU Council Common Position 2007/140/CFSP | February 27, 2007 | Commander of the IRGC Air Force; involved in Iran's ballistic missile program |
| | U.S. Treasury, Executive Order 13382 | October 25, 2007 | Commander of the IRGC Air Force |
| **Behnam Shahriyari** | U.S. Treasury, Executive Order 13224 | June 23, 2011 | Designated for acting on behalf of Liner Transport Kish (LTK), an IRGC-linked shipping company |
| **Brigadier General Ali Shamshiri** | EU Council Decision of June 23, 2008 Implementing Article 7(2) of Regulation (EC) No. 423/2007 | June 24, 2008 | MODAFL Deputy for Counter-Intelligence, responsible for security of MODAFL personnel and Installations |
| **Brigadier General Qasem Soleimani** | UNSC Resolution 1747 | March 24, 2007 | Commander of the Qods Force |
| | EU Commission Regulation No. 441/2007 | April 20, 2007 | Commander of the Qods Force |
| | U.S. Treasury, Executive Order 13382 | October 25, 2007 | Commander of the Qods Force |
| **Hossein Taeb** | U.S. Treasury, Executive Order 13553 | September 29, 2010 | Deputy IRGC Commander for Intelligence; designated for human rights violations in the aftermath of the June 2009 elections |
| **Brigadier-General Ahmad Vahidi** | EU Council Decision of June 23, 2008 Implementing Article 7(2) of Regulation (EC) No. 423/2007 | June 24, 2008 | Deputy Head of MODAFL |

| IRGC Affiliated Individuals | Authority & Legislation | Designation Date | Reason for Designation |
|---|---|---|---|
| **Brigadier General Mohammad Reza Zahedi** | UNSC Resolution 1747 | March 24, 2007 | Commander of IRGC Ground Forces |
| | EU Commission Regulation No. 441/2007 | April 20, 2007 | Commander of the IRGC Ground Forces |
| | U.S. Treasury, Executive Order 13224 | August 3, 2010 | Commander of IRGC Qods Forces in Lebanon; plays a key role in supporting Hezbollah |
| **General Zolqadr** | UNSC Resolution 1747 | March 24, 2007 | IRGC officer, Deputy Interior Minister for Security Affairs |
| | EU Commission Regulation No. 441/2007 | April 20, 2007 | IRGC officer, Deputy Interior Minister for Security Affairs |

# Designation of IRISL Companies by the U.S. and EU

| IRISL Company | Authority & Legislation | Designation Date | Reason for Designation |
|---|---|---|---|
| Islamic Republic of Iran Shipping Lines (IRISL) | U.S. Treasury, Executive Order 13382 | September 10, 2008 | IRISL provides logistical services to Iran's Ministry of Defense and Armed Forces Logistics (MODAFL). |
| | UNSC Resolution 1929 | June 9, 2010 | |
| Advance Novel | U.S. Treasury, Executive Order 13382 | January 13, 2011 | |
| | EU Commission Regulation No. 503/2011 | May 23, 2011 | Hong Kong-based company owned by Mill Dene Ltd. |
| Alpha Effort Ltd. | U.S. Treasury, Executive Order 13382 | January 13, 2011 | |
| | EU Commission Regulation No. 503/2011 | May 23, 2011 | Hong Kong-based company owned by Mill Dene Ltd. |
| Ashtead Shipping Company Ltd. | U.S. Treasury, Executive Order 13382 | November 30, 2010 | IRISL front company located on the Isle of Man; It is 100 percent owned by IRISL and is the registered owner of a vessel owned by IRISL or an IRISL affiliate. |
| | EU Commission Regulation No. 503/2011 | May 23, 2011 | |
| Asia Marine Networks Pte. Ltd | U.S. Treasury, Executive Order 13382 | September 10, 2008 | Singapore-based IRISL affiliate |

| IRISL Company | Authority & Legislation | Designation Date | Reason for Designation |
|---|---|---|---|
| Atlantic Intermodal | U.S. Treasury, Executive Order 13382 | June 20, 2011 | Acts on behalf of IRISL affiliate Oasis Freight Agency and/or IRISL |
| Azores Shipping | U.S. Treasury, Executive Order 13382 | June 20, 2011 | Acts on behalf of IRISL affiliate Oasis Freight Agency and/or IRISL |
| Best Precise Ltd. | U.S. Treasury, Executive Order 13382 | January 13, 2011 | |
| | EU Commission Regulation No. 503/2011 | May 23, 2011 | Hong Kong-based company owned by Mill Dene Ltd. |
| Byfleet Shipping Company Ltd. | U.S. Treasury, Executive Order 13382 | November 30, 2010 | |
| | EU Commission Regulation No. 503/2011 | May 23, 2011 | IRISL front company located on the Isle of Man; It is 100 percent owned by IRISL and is the registered owner of a vessel owned by IRISL or an IRISL affiliate. |
| CISCO Shipping Co. Ltd | U.S. Treasury, Executive Order 13382 | September 10, 2008 | Owned or controlled by IRISL |
| Cobham Shipping Company Ltd. | U.S. Treasury, Executive Order 13382 | November 30, 2010 | |
| | EU Commission Regulation No. 503/2011 | May 23, 2011 | IRISL front company located on the Isle of Man; It is 100 percent owned by IRISL and is the registered owner of a vessel owned by IRISL or an IRISL affiliate. |
| Concept Giant Ltd. | U.S. Treasury, Executive Order 13382 | January 13, 2011 | |
| | EU Commission Regulation No. 503/2011 | May 23, 2011 | Hong Kong-based company owned by Mill Dene Ltd. |
| Crystal Shipping | U.S. Treasury, Executive Order 13382 | June 20, 2011 | Acts on behalf of IRISL affiliate Oasis Freight Agency and/or IRISL |
| Darya Capital Administration GmbH | U.S. Treasury, Executive Order 13382 | October 27, 2010 | Wholly-owned subsidiary of IRISL Europe GmbH |
| | EU Commission Regulation No. 503/2011 | May 23, 2011 | |

| IRISL Company | Authority & Legislation | Designation Date | Reason for Designation |
|---|---|---|---|
| **Dorking Shipping Company Ltd.** | U.S. Treasury, Executive Order 13382 | November 30, 2010 | |
| | EU Commission Regulation No. 503/2011 | May 23, 2011 | IRISL front company located on the Isle of Man; It is 100 percent owned by IRISL and is the registered owner of a vessel owned by IRISL or an IRISL affiliate. |
| **Effingham Shipping Company Ltd.** | U.S. Treasury, Executive Order 13382 | November 30, 2010 | |
| | EU Commission Regulation No. 503/2011 | May 23, 2011 | IRISL front company located on the Isle of Man; It is 100 percent owned by IRISL and is the registered owner of a vessel owned by IRISL or an IRISL affiliate. |
| **Eighth Ocean Administration GmbH** | U.S. Treasury, Executive Order 13382 | October 27, 2010 | |
| | EU Commission Regulation No. 503/2011 | May 23, 2011 | Owned or controlled by IRISL |
| **Eighth Ocean GmbH & Co. Kg** | U.S. Treasury, Executive Order 13382 | October 27, 2010 | |
| | EU Commission Regulation No. 503/2011 | May 23, 2011 | Owned or controlled by IRISL |
| **Eleventh Ocean Administration GmbH** | U.S. Treasury, Executive Order 13382 | October 27, 2010 | |
| | EU Commission Regulation No. 503/2011 | May 23, 2011 | Owned or controlled by IRISL |
| **Eleventh Ocean GmbH & Co. Kg** | U.S. Treasury, Executive Order 13382 | October 27, 2010 | |
| | EU Commission Regulation No. 503/2011 | May 23, 2011 | Owned or controlled by IRISL |

| IRISL Company | Authority & Legislation | Designation Date | Reason for Designation |
|---|---|---|---|
| Farnham Shipping Company Ltd. | U.S. Treasury, Executive Order 13382 | November 30, 2010 | |
| | EU Commission Regulation No. 503/2011 | May 23, 2011 | IRISL front company located on the Isle of Man; It is 100 percent owned by IRISL and is the registered owner of a vessel owned by IRISL or an IRISL affiliate. |
| Fairway Shipping | U.S. Treasury, Executive Order 13382 | June 20, 2011 | U.K.-based affiliate of IRISL |
| Fifteenth Ocean Administration GmbH | U.S. Treasury, Executive Order 13382 | October 27, 2010 | Owned or controlled by IRISL |
| | EU Commission Regulation No. 503/2011 | May 23, 2011 | |
| Fifteenth Ocean GmbH & Co. Kg | U.S. Treasury, Executive Order 13382 | October 27, 2010 | Owned or controlled by IRISL |
| | EU Commission Regulation No. 503/2011 | May 23, 2011 | |
| Fifth Ocean Administration GmbH | U.S. Treasury, Executive Order 13382 | October 27, 2010 | Owned or controlled by IRISL |
| | EU Commission Regulation No. 503/2011 | May 23, 2011 | |
| Fifth Ocean GmbH & Co. Kg | U.S. Treasury, Executive Order 13382 | October 27, 2010 | Owned or controlled by IRISL |
| | EU Commission Regulation No. 503/2011 | May 23, 2011 | |
| First Ocean Administration GmbH | U.S. Treasury, Executive Order 13382 | October 27, 2010 | Owned or controlled by IRISL |
| | EU Commission Regulation No. 503/2011 | May 23, 2011 | |
| First Ocean GmbH & Co. Kg | U.S. Treasury, Executive Order 13382 | October 27, 2010 | Owned or controlled by IRISL |
| | EU Commission Regulation No. 503/2011 | May 23, 2011 | |

| IRISL Company | Authority & Legislation | Designation Date | Reason for Designation |
|---|---|---|---|
| Fourteenth Ocean Administration GmbH | U.S. Treasury, Executive Order 13382 | October 27, 2010 | Owned or controlled by IRISL |
| | EU Commission Regulation No. 503/2011 | May 23, 2011 | |
| Fourteenth Ocean GmbH & Co. Kg | U.S. Treasury, Executive Order 13382 | October 27, 2010 | Owned or controlled by IRISL |
| | EU Commission Regulation No. 503/2011 | May 23, 2011 | |
| Fourth Ocean Administration GmbH | U.S. Treasury, Executive Order 13382 | October 27, 2010 | Owned or controlled by IRISL |
| | EU Commission Regulation No. 503/2011 | May 23, 2011 | |
| Fourth Ocean GmbH & Co. Kg | U.S. Treasury, Executive Order 13382 | October 27, 2010 | Owned or controlled by IRISL |
| | EU Commission Regulation No. 503/2011 | May 23, 2011 | |
| Gomshall Shipping Company Ltd. | U.S. Treasury, Executive Order 13382 | November 30, 2010 | |
| | EU Commission Regulation No. 503/2011 | May 23, 2011 | IRISL front company located on the Isle of Man; It is 100 percent owned by IRISL and is the registered owner of a vessel owned by IRISL or an IRISL affiliate. |
| Great Method Ltd. | U.S. Treasury, Executive Order 13382 | January 13, 2011 | |
| | EU Commission Regulation No. 503/2011 | May 23, 2011 | Hong Kong-based company owned by Mill Dene Ltd. |
| Great Ocean Shipping Services | U.S. Treasury, Executive Order 13382 | June 20, 2011 | Acts on behalf of IRISL affiliate Oasis Freight Agency and/or IRISL |
| Hafiz Darya Shipping Company | U.S. Treasury, Executive Order 13382 | June 16, 2010 | IRISL front company based out of Tehran, Iran |

| IRISL Company | Authority & Legislation | Designation Date | Reason for Designation |
|---|---|---|---|
| Horsham Shipping Company Ltd. | U.S. Treasury, Executive Order 13382 | November 30, 2010 | |
| | EU Commission Regulation No. 503/2011 | May 23, 2011 | IRISL front company located on the Isle of Man; It is 100 percent owned by IRISL and is the registered owner of a vessel owned by IRISL or an IRISL affiliate. |
| HTTS Hanseatic Trade Trust and Shipping Gmbh | U.S. Treasury, Executive Order 13382 | October 27, 2010 | |
| Ideal Success Investments Ltd. | U.S. Treasury, Executive Order 13382 | January 13, 2011 | Hong Kong-based company owned by individuals acting on behalf of IRISL |
| Insight World Ltd. | EU Commission Regulation No. 503/2011 | May 23, 2011 | Hong Kong-based company owned by Loweswater Ltd. |
| Iran o Misr Shipping Co. | U.S. Treasury, Executive Order 13382 | September 10, 2008 | Owned or controlled by IRISL |
| Iran o Hind Shipping Co. | U.S. Treasury, Executive Order 13382 | September 10, 2008 | Owned or controlled by IRISL |
| | UNSC Resolution 1929 | June 9, 2010 | |
| Irinvestship Ltd | U.S. Treasury, Executive Order 13382 | September 10, 2008 | Owned or controlled by IRISL |
| Irital Shipping SRL Co. | U.S. Treasury, Executive Order 13382 | September 10, 2008 | Owned or controlled by IRISL |
| | UNSC Resolution 1929 | June 9, 2010 | |
| IRISL Benelux NV | U.S. Treasury, Executive Order 13382 | September 10, 2008 | Owned or controlled by IRISL |
| | UNSC Resolution 1929 | June 9, 2010 | |
| IRISL China Shipping Co. Ltd | U.S. Treasury, Executive Order 13382 | September 10, 2008 | Owned or controlled by IRISL |
| IRISL Europe Gmbh | U.S. Treasury, Executive Order 13382 | September 10, 2008 | Owned or controlled by IRISL |

| IRISL Company | Authority & Legislation | Designation Date | Reason for Designation |
|---|---|---|---|
| IRISL (Malta) Ltd | U.S. Treasury, Executive Order 13382 | September 10, 2008 | Owned or controlled by IRISL |
| IRISL Marine Services and Engineering Company | U.S. Treasury, Executive Order 13382 | September 10, 2008 | |
| IRISL Multimodal Transport Co. | U.S. Treasury, Executive Order 13382 | September 10, 2008 | Owned or controlled by IRISL |
| Kerman Shipping Company Ltd. | U.S. Treasury, Executive Order 13382 | October 27, 2010 | Wholly-owned subsidiary of IRISL |
| | EU Commission Regulation No. 503/2011 | May 23, 2011 | |
| Khazar Sea Shipping Lines | U.S. Treasury, Executive Order 13382 | September 10, 2008 | Owned or controlled by IRISL |
| Kingdom New Ltd. | EU Commission Regulation No. 503/2011 | May 23, 2011 | Hong Kong-based company owned by Loweswater Ltd. |
| Lancelin Shipping Company Ltd. | U.S. Treasury, Executive Order 13382 | October 27, 2010 | Wholly-owned by IRISL |
| | EU Commission Regulation No. 503/2011 | May 23, 2011 | |
| Leading Maritime PTE Ltd. | U.S. Treasury, Executive Order 13382 | June 20, 2011 | IRISL front company |
| Logistic Smart Ltd. | U.S. Treasury, Executive Order 13382 | January 13, 2011 | Hong Kong-based company owned by Loweswater Ltd. |
| | EU Commission Regulation No. 503/2011 | May 23, 2011 | |

| IRISL Company | Authority & Legislation | Designation Date | Reason for Designation |
|---|---|---|---|
| Loweswater Ltd. | U.S. Treasury, Executive Order 13382 | January 13, 2011 | |
| | EU Commission Regulation No. 503/2011 | May 23, 2011 | Isle of Man-administered company that controls ship-owning companies in Hong Kong; The ships are operated by EU-sanctioned Safiran Payam Darya Shipping Lines that took over IRISL's bulk services and routes and uses vessels previously owned by IRISL. |
| Maraner Holdings Ltd | U.S. Treasury, Executive Order 13382 | February 2, 2011 | |
| Moallem Insurance Co. | U.S. Treasury, Executive Order 13382 | December 21, 2010 | Provides maritime insurance for IRISL |
| Mill Dene Ltd. | U.S. Treasury, Executive Order 13382 | January 13, 2011 | IRISL subsidiary based in Malta |
| | EU Commission Regulation No. 503/2011 | May 23, 2011 | Isle of Man-administered company that controls ship-owning companies in Hong Kong; The ships are operated by EU-sanctioned Safiran Payam Darya Shipping Lines that took over IRISL's bulk services and routes and uses vessels previously owned by IRISL. |
| Nari Shipping and Chartering GmbH & Co. KG | U.S. Treasury, Executive Order 13382 | October 27, 2010 | |
| | EU Commission Regulation No. 503/2011 | May 23, 2011 | Owned by Ocean Capital Administration and IRISL Europe |
| Neuman Ltd. | U.S. Treasury, Executive Order 13382 | January 13, 2011 | |
| | EU Commission Regulation No. 503/2011 | May 23, 2011 | Hong Kong-based company owned by Loweswater Ltd. |

EMANUELE OTTOLENGHI

| IRISL Company | Authority & Legislation | Designation Date | Reason for Designation |
|---|---|---|---|
| **New Desire Ltd.** | U.S. Treasury, Executive Order 13382 | January 13, 2011 | |
| | EU Commission Regulation No. 503/2011 | May 23, 2011 | Hong Kong-based company owned by Loweswater Ltd. |
| **New Synergy Ltd.** | EU Commission Regulation No. 503/2011 | May 23, 2011 | Hong Kong-based company owned by Springthorpe Ltd. |
| **Ninth Ocean Administration GmbH** | U.S. Treasury, Executive Order 13382 | October 27, 2010 | Owned or controlled by IRISL |
| | EU Commission Regulation No. 503/2011 | May 23, 2011 | |
| **Ninth Ocean GmbH & Co. Kg** | U.S. Treasury, Executive Order 13382 | October 27, 2010 | Owned or controlled by IRISL |
| | EU Commission Regulation No. 503/2011 | May 23, 2011 | |
| **Oasis Freight Agencies** | U.S. Treasury, Executive Order 13382 | September 10, 2008 | Owned or controlled by IRISL |
| **Ocean Capital Administration GmbH** | U.S. Treasury, Executive Order 13382 | October 27, 2010 | A German-based IRISL holding company that, together with IRISL Europe, owns Nari Shipping and Chartering GmbH and Co. KG |
| | EU Commission Regulation No. 503/2011 | May 23, 2011 | |
| **Pacific Shipping** | U.S. Treasury, Executive Order 13382 | June 20, 2011 | Acts on behalf of IRISL affiliate Oasis Freight Agency and/or IRISL |
| **Partner Century Ltd.** | U.S. Treasury, Executive Order 13382 | January 13, 2011 | Hong Kong-based company owned by Springthorpe Ltd. |
| | EU Commission Regulation No. 503/2011 | May 23, 2011 | |
| **Pearl Shipping** | U.S. Treasury, Executive Order 13382 | June 20, 2011 | Acts on behalf of IRISL affiliate Oasis Freight Agency and/or IRISL |
| **Royal-Med Shipping Agency Ltd.** | U.S. Treasury, Executive Order 13382 | February 2, 2011 | Malta-based IRISL subsidiary |

| IRISL Company | Authority & Legislation | Designation Date | Reason for Designation |
|---|---|---|---|
| Sackville Holdings Ltd. | U.S. Treasury, Executive Order 13382 | January 13, 2011 | Hong Kong-based company owned by Springthorpe Ltd. |
| | EU Commission Regulation No. 503/2011 | May 23, 2011 | |
| Safiran Payam Darya (SAPID) Shipping Co. | U.S. Treasury, Executive Order 13382 | June 16, 2010 | IRISL front company, created in 2009 to handle bulk and general cargo operations |
| Sandford Group Ltd. | U.S. Treasury, Executive Order 13382 | January 13, 2011 | Hong Kong-based company owned by Springthorpe Ltd. |
| | EU Commission Regulation No. 503/2011 | May 23, 2011 | |
| Santex Lines | U.S. Treasury, Executive Order 13382 | January 13, 2011 | IRISL regional office in China |
| Second Ocean Administration GmbH | U.S. Treasury, Executive Order 13382 | October 27, 2010 | Owned or controlled by IRISL |
| | EU Commission Regulation No. 503/2011 | May 23, 2011 | IRISL affiliated company based out of Hong Kong |
| Second Ocean GmbH & Co. Kg | EU Commission Regulation No. 503/2011 | May 23, 2011 | Owned or controlled by IRISL |
| Seibow Logistics Ltd. | U.S. Treasury, Executive Order 13382 | June 16, 2010 | |
| Seventh Ocean Administration GmbH | U.S. Treasury, Executive Order 13382 | October 27, 2010 | Owned or controlled by IRISL |
| | EU Commission Regulation No. 503/2011 | May 23, 2011 | |
| Seventh Ocean GmbH & Co. Kg | U.S. Treasury, Executive Order 13382 | October 27, 2010 | Owned or controlled by IRISL |
| | EU Commission Regulation No. 503/2011 | May 23, 2011 | |

| IRISL Company | Authority & Legislation | Designation Date | Reason for Designation |
|---|---|---|---|
| **Shallon Ltd.** | U.S. Treasury, Executive Order 13382 | January 13, 2011 | |
| | EU Commission Regulation No. 503/2011 | May 23, 2011 | Isle of Man-administered company that controls ship-owning companies in Hong Kong; The ships are operated by EU-sanctioned Safiran Payam Darya Shipping Lines that took over IRISL's bulk services and routes and uses vessels previously owned by IRISL. |
| **Shere Shipping Company Ltd.** | U.S. Treasury, Executive Order 13382 | October 27, 2010 | Wholly-owned subsidiary of Woking Shipping Investments Ltd., which is a subsidiary of IRISL |
| | EU Commission Regulation No. 503/2011 | May 23, 2011 | |
| **Shipping Computer Services Company** | U.S. Treasury, Executive Order 13382 | September 10, 2008 | Owned or controlled by IRISL |
| **Sino Access Limited** | U.S. Treasury, Executive Order 13382 | January 13, 2011 | Hong Kong-based company owned by Springthorpe Ltd. |
| | EU Commission Regulation No. 503/2011 | May 23, 2011 | |
| **Sinose Maritime** | U.S. Treasury, Executive Order 13382 | January 13, 2011 | Agent of Asian marine Network and IRISL Singapore |
| **Sixteenth Ocean Administration GmbH** | EU Commission Regulation No. 503/2011 | May 23, 2011 | Owned or controlled by IRISL |
| **Sixteenth Ocean GmbH & Co. Kg** | EU Commission Regulation No. 503/2011 | May 23, 2011 | Owned or controlled by IRISL |
| **Sixth Ocean Administration GmbH** | U.S. Treasury, Executive Order 13382 | October 27, 2010 | Owned or controlled by IRISL |
| | EU Commission Regulation No. 503/2011 | May 23, 2011 | |

| IRISL Company | Authority & Legislation | Designation Date | Reason for Designation |
|---|---|---|---|
| Sixth Ocean GmbH & Co. Kg | U.S. Treasury, Executive Order 13382 | October 27, 2010 | Owned or controlled by IRISL |
| | EU Commission Regulation No. 503/2011 | May 23, 2011 | |
| Smart Day Holdings Ltd. | U.S. Treasury, Executive Order 13382 | January 13, 2011 | |
| | EU Commission Regulation No. 503/2011 | May 23, 2011 | Hong Kong-based company owned by Shallon Ltd. |
| South Shipping Line Iran | U.S. Treasury, Executive Order 13382 | September 10, 2008 | Owned or controlled by IRISL |
| | UNSC Resolution 1929 | June 9, 2010 | |
| Soroush Sarzam Asatir Ship Management Co. | U.S. Treasury, Executive Order 13382 | June 16, 2010 | IRISL front company located in Tehran; shares corporate offices with IRISL |
| Springthorpe Ltd. | U.S. Treasury, Executive Order 13382 | January 13, 2011 | |
| | EU Commission Regulation No. 503/2011 | May 23, 2011 | Isle of Man-administered company that controls ship-owning companies in Hong Kong; The ships are operated by EU-sanctioned Safiran Payam Darya Shipping Lines that took over IRISL's bulk services and routes and uses vessels previously owned by IRISL. |
| Starry Shine International Ltd. | U.S. Treasury, Executive Order 13382 | January 13, 2011 | Hong Kong-based company owned by individuals acting on behalf of IRISL |
| System Wise Ltd. (a.k.a. System Wise Ltd.) | U.S. Treasury, Executive Order 13382 | January 13, 2011 | Hong Kong-based company owned by Shallon Ltd. |
| | EU Commission Regulation No. 503/2011 | May 23, 2011 | |
| Tenth Ocean Administration GmbH | EU Commission Regulation No. 503/2011 | May 23, 2011 | Owned or controlled by IRISL |

| IRISL Company | Authority & Legislation | Designation Date | Reason for Designation |
|---|---|---|---|
| Tenth Ocean GmbH & Co. Kg | U.S. Treasury, Executive Order 13382 | October 27, 2010 | |
| | EU Commission Regulation No. 503/2011 | May 23, 2011 | Owned or controlled by IRISL |
| Third Ocean Administration GmbH | U.S. Treasury, Executive Order 13382 | October 27, 2010 | |
| | EU Commission Regulation No. 503/2011 | May 23, 2011 | Owned or controlled by IRISL |
| Third Ocean GmbH & Co. Kg | U.S. Treasury, Executive Order 13382 | October 27, 2010 | |
| | EU Commission Regulation No. 503/2011 | May 23, 2011 | Owned or controlled by IRISL |
| Thirteenth Ocean Administration GmbH | EU Commission Regulation No. 503/2011 | May 23, 2011 | Owned or controlled by IRISL |
| Thirteenth Ocean GmbH & Co. Kg | U.S. Treasury, Executive Order 13382 | October 27, 2010 | |
| | EU Commission Regulation No. 503/2011 | May 23, 2011 | Owned or controlled by IRISL |
| Tongham Shipping Company Ltd. | U.S. Treasury, Executive Order 13382 | October 27, 2010 | Wholly-owned subsidiary of Woking Shipping Investments Ltd., which is a subsidiary of IRISL |
| | EU Commission Regulation No. 503/2011 | May 23, 2011 | |
| Top Glacier Company Ltd | U.S. Treasury, Executive Order 13382 | January 13, 2011 | Hong Kong-based company owned by individuals acting on behalf of IRISL |
| Top Prestige Trading Limited | U.S. Treasury, Executive Order 13382 | January 13, 2011 | Hong Kong-based company owned by individuals acting on behalf of IRISL |

| IRISL Company | Authority & Legislation | Designation Date | Reason for Designation |
|---|---|---|---|
| Trade Treasure Limited | U.S. Treasury, Executive Order 13382 | January 13, 2011 | Hong Kong-based company owned by Shallon Ltd. |
| | EU Commission Regulation No. 503/2011 | May 23, 2011 | |
| True Honour Holdings Ltd. | U.S. Treasury, Executive Order 13382 | January 13, 2011 | |
| | EU Commission Regulation No. 503/2011 | May 23, 2011 | Hong Kong-based company owned by Shallon Ltd. |
| Twelfth Ocean Administration GmbH | U.S. Treasury, Executive Order 13382 | October 27, 2010 | |
| | EU Commission Regulation No. 503/2011 | May 23, 2011 | Owned or controlled by IRISL |
| Twelfth Ocean GmbH & Co. Kg | U.S. Treasury, Executive Order 13382 | October 27, 2010 | |
| | EU Commission Regulation No. 503/2011 | May 23, 2011 | Owned or controlled by IRISL |
| Uppercourt Shipping Company Ltd | U.S. Treasury, Executive Order 13382 | October 27, 2010 | |
| | EU Commission Regulation No. 503/2011 | May 23, 2011 | Wholly-owned subsidiary of Woking Shipping Investments Ltd., which is a subsidiary of IRISL |
| Valfajr 8th Shipping Line Co SSK | U.S. Treasury, Executive Order 13382 | September 10, 2008 | Owned or controlled by IRISL |
| Vobster Shipping Company | U.S. Treasury, Executive Order 13382 | October 27, 2010 | |
| | EU Commission Regulation No. 503/2011 | May 23, 2011 | Wholly-owned subsidiary of Woking Shipping Investments Ltd., which is a subsidiary of IRISL |
| Woking Shipping Investments Ltd. | U.S. Treasury, Executive Order 13382 | October 27, 2010 | |
| | EU Commission Regulation No. 503/2011 | May 23, 2011 | Owned or controlled by IRISL |

# Designations of IRISL Ships

The United States designated the Islamic Republic of Iran Shipping Lines (IRISL) in September 2008 for its involvement in Iran's missile programs. In an effort to circumvent these restrictions, IRISL has developed a vast web of front companies, and it continues to change the names of the company's ships. However, it is impossible for ship owners to change their ships' International Maritime Organization (IMO) number, which is a seven digit code assigned to all ships when they are built. Thus, while IRISL is continually changing the names of its ships, it is possible to track these vessels, thereby restricting IRISL's ability to deceive.

| IMO | Current Name | Former Name | Flag |
|---|---|---|---|
| 7027899 | Mirza Kochek Khan | N/A | Iran |
| 7375363 | Hootan | Iran Sepah | Iran |
| 7389792 | Iran Beheshti | N/A | Iran |
| 7428809 | Despina | Iran Kolahdooz | Iran |
| 7620550 | Gomidas | Iran Esteghlal | Iran |
| 7632814 | Assa | Iran Entekhab | Iran |
| 7632826 | Amitees | Iran Jomhuri | Iran |
| 7904580 | Hormuz 2 | N/A | Iran |
| 8105284 | Parmida | Iran Afzal | Iran |
| 8107579 | Markarid | Iran Deyanat | Iran |
| 8107581 | Barsam | Iran Shariat | Iran |
| 8108559 | Pantea | Iran Adl | Iran |
| 8112990 | Tabak | Iran Amanat | Iran |
| 8113009 | Iran Akhavan | N/A | Iran |
| 8113011 | Iran Sarbaz | N/A | Iran |
| 8203608 | Iran Sahar | Ra-Ees Ali; Sarina | Iran |
| 8215742 | Sabrina | Iran Basheer | Iran |
| 8309593 | Attribute | Iran Diamond; Diamond | Hong Kong |

| IMO | Current Name | Former Name | Flag |
|-----|--------------|-------------|------|
| 8309608 | Alias | Iran Devotee; Devotee | Hong Kong |
| 8309610 | Aquarian | Dignified; Iran Dignified | Hong Kong |
| 8309622 | Adventist | Iran Madani | Hong Kong |
| 8309634 | Agean | Dynamize; Iran Dynamize | Hong Kong |
| 8309646 | Angel | Dapper; Iran Dapper | Hong Kong |
| 8309658 | Agile | Decorous; Iran Decorous | Hong Kong |
| 8309672 | Ajax | Iran Ghazi; Dynasty | Hong Kong |
| 8309684 | Acrobat | Devotional; Iran Devotional | Hong Kong |
| 8309696 | Admiral | Dais; Iran Dais | Hong Kong |
| 8309701 | Amplify | Diplomat; Iran Diplomat | Hong Kong |
| 8314263 | Iran Hormuz 21 | N/A | Iran |
| 8314275 | Iran Hormuz 22 | N/A | Iran |
| 8319782 | Iran Hormuz 23 | N/A | Iran |
| 8320121 | Aerolite | Delegate; Iran Delegate | Hong Kong |
| 8320133 | Adrian | Delight; Iran Delight; Iran Jamal | Hong Kong |
| 8320145 | Apollo | Iran Navab; Iran Destiny | Hong Kong |
| 8320157 | Anil | Dandy; Iran Dandy | Hong Kong |
| 8320169 | Accurate | Drifter; Iran Drifter | Hong Kong |
| 8320171 | Atrium | Diamond; Iran Hamzeh | Hong Kong |
| 8320183 | Atlantic | Iran Dreamland; Dreamland | Hong Kong |
| 8320195 | Alameda | Iran Dolphin | Hong Kong |
| 8422072 | Iran Hormuz 25 | N/A | Iran |
| 8422084 | Iran Hormuz 26 | N/A | Iran |
| 8605234 | Dorita | Iran Moein | Iran |
| 8820925 | Iran Shalamcheh | N/A | Iran |
| 8984484 | AAJ | N/A | Iran |
| 9005596 | Iran Hormuz 12 | N/A | Iran |
| 9007582 | Iran Kong | N/A | Iran |
| 9010711 | Vista | Iran Baseer | Iran |
| 9010723 | Viana | Iran Ghadeer | Iran |
| 9020778 | Iran Hormuz 14 | N/A | Iran |
| 9040479 | Sattar | N/A | Malta |
| 9051624 | Abba | Iran Matin | Iran |
| 9051636 | Mulberry | Iran Brilliance; Brilliance | Malta |
| 9051648 | Marigold | Iran Brightness; Brightness | Malta |
| 9051650 | Margrave | Iran Brave | Malta |
| 9071519 | Negeen | N/A | Iran |
| 9074092 | Attar | N/A | Malta |

| IMO | Current Name | Former Name | Flag |
|---|---|---|---|
| 9076478 | Iran Kabeer | N/A | Iran |
| 9101649 | Teen | N/A | Malta |
| 9103087 | Gowhar | N/A | Iran |
| 9118513 | Mekong Spirit | N/A | Cyprus |
| 9118551 | Iran Daleer | N/A | Iran |
| 9137210 | Patris | N/A | Malta |
| 9137246 | Ferdos | Nardis | Iran |
| 9137258 | Kados | Iran Sahel | Iran |
| 9138044 | Zomoroud | N/A | Iran |
| 9138056 | Brelyan | N/A | Iran |
| 9165786 | Gabion | Seventh Ocean | Malta |
| 9165798 | Galax | Ninth Ocean | Malta |
| 9165803 | Eighth Ocean | N/A | Malta |
| 9165815 | Gladiolus | Tenth Ocean | Malta |
| 9165827 | Goldenrod | Iran Lucky Lily; Lucky Lily | Malta |
| 9165839 | Garland | Iran Lucky Man; Lucky Man | Malta |
| 9167253 | Lantana | Ocean Candle; Iran Ocean Candle | Malta |
| 9167265 | Lilied | Iran Sea State; Sea State | Malta |
| 9167277 | Lavendar | Iran Pretty Sea; Pretty Sea | Malta |
| 9167289 | Limnetic | Sea Flower | Malta |
| 9167291 | Lodestar | Sea Bloom; Iran Sea Bloom | Malta |
| 9184691 | Iran Shahed | N/A | Iran |
| 9193185 | Nafis | Iran Azarbayjan; ZAWA | Cyprus |
| 9193197 | Mazandaran | Iran Mazandaran | Malta |
| 9193202 | Bluebell | Iran Gilan | Malta |
| 9193214 | Dorsan | Iran Khorasan; Khorasan | Malta |
| 9209324 | Daffodil | Eleventh Ocean | Malta |
| 9209336 | Dandelion | New State | Malta |
| 9209348 | Dandle | Twelfth Ocean | Malta |
| 9209350 | Silver Craft | Iran Kerman | Malta |
| 9213387 | Atena | Iran Yazd; Lancelin | Cyprus |
| 9213399 | Acena | Iran Kermanshah | Cyprus |
| 9226944 | Golestan | Iran Golestan | Malta |
| 9226956 | Hamadan | Iran Hamadan | Malta |
| 9245304 | Iran Darya | N/A | Iran |
| 9260160 | ZAR | N/A | Iran |
| 9260172 | Zivar | N/A | Iran |

| IMO | Current Name | Former Name | Flag |
|---|---|---|---|
| 9270646 | Valili | Iran Arak | Malta |
| 9270658 | Silver Zone | Iran Bushehr | Malta |
| 9270696 | Iran Kashan | N/A | Iran |
| 9274941 | Sinin | N/A | Malta |
| 9283007 | Parmis | Iran Piroozi; SAKAS | Barbados |
| 9283007 | Sakas | Iran Piroozi; Sakas I; Sakas IT; Sakas BBB; Sakas D 2; Sakas D8; Sakas JA | Iran |
| 9283019 | Armis | Iran Zanjan; Visea | Barbados |
| 9283021 | Salis | Iran Fars; Sewak; Sewak ET; Sewak LZ; Sewak D; Sewak IT; Sewak I; Sewak IBB; | Barbados |
| 9283033 | Hadis | Iran Ilam; Sepitam | Barbados |
| 9284142 | Pardis | Iran Yasooj; SIMBER | Barbados |
| 9284154 | Tandis | Iran Ardebil; SEPANTA | Barbados |
| 9305192 | Shere | Iran Tabas | Malta |
| 9305207 | Uppercourt | Iran Bojnoord | Malta |
| 9305219 | Tongham | Iran Birjand | Malta |
| 9305221 | Vobster | Iran Persian Gulf; Persian Gulf | Malta |
| 9323833 | Horsham | Iran Bam | Malta |
| 9328900 | Sahand | Iran Sahand | Malta |
| 9346524 | Sabalan | Iran Sabalan | Malta |
| 9346536 | Tuchal | Iran Tuchal | Malta |
| 9346548 | Palmary | Iran Zagros; Zagros | Malta |
| 9349576 | First Ocean | N/A | Malta |
| 9349588 | Second Ocean | N/A | Malta |
| 9349590 | Third Ocean | N/A | Malta |
| 9349667 | Decker | Fifth Ocean | Malta |
| 9349679 | Decretive | Sixth Ocean | Malta |
| 9367982 | Iran Anzali | N/A | Iran |
| 9367994 | Sania | Iran Nowshahr | Iran |
| 9368003 | Sarir | Iran Amirabad | Iran |
| 9368015 | Somia | Iran Torkaman | Iran |
| 9369710 | Glory | N/A | Malta |
| 9369722 | Graceful | N/A | Malta |
| 9379636 | Abtin 1 | N/A | Iran |
| 9386500 | Chastity | Iran Shaafi; Shaafi | Malta |
| 9387786 | Chimes | Iran Vaafi; Vaafi | Malta |

| IMO | Current Name | Former Name | Flag |
|------|--------------|-------------|------|
| 9387798 | Haadi | N/A | Malta |
| 9387803 | Raazi | N/A | Malta |
| 9387815 | Saei | N/A | Malta |
| 9405930 | Baaghi | N/A | Malta |
| 9405942 | Aali | N/A | Malta |
| 9405954 | Baani | N/A | Malta |
| 9405966 | Haami | N/A | Malta |
| 9405978 | Shaadi | N/A | Malta |
| 9420356 | Shayan 1 | N/A | Iran |
| 9420368 | Taban 1 | N/A | Iran |
| 9420370 | Samin 1 | N/A | Malta |
| 9465746 | Chaplet | Iran Rahim; Rahim | Malta |
| 9465758 | Chariot | Iran Karim; Karim | Malta |
| 9465760 | Azim | Iran Azim; Chapman | Malta |
| 9465849 | Chairman | Alim; Iran Alim | Malta |
| 9465851 | Salim | N/A | Malta |
| 9465863 | Chaparel | Hakim; Iran Hakim; DI Ali | Malta |

## BIBLIOGRAPHY

## B O O K S

Hamid Algar, *Islam and Revolution Writings and Declarations of Imam Khomeini (1941-1980)*. (North Haledon, NJ: Mizan Press, 1981).

Ali Ansari, *Crisis of Authority: Iran's 2009 Presidential Elections*. (Washington, D.C.: Chatham House, 2010).

Robert Baer, *The Devil We Know*. (NY: Three Rivers Press, 2008).

Mark Bowden, *Guests of the Ayatollah*. (NY: Grove Press, 2006).

Louis J. Freeh, *My FBI Bringing Down the Mafia, Investigating Bill Clinton and Fighting the War on Terror*. (Waterville, ME: Thorndike Press, 2006).

Bruce Hoffman, *Inside Terrorism*. (NY: Columbia University Press, 1999).

David Menashri, "Iran's Revolutionary Politics: Islam and National Identity," in Leonard Binder (Ed.), *Ethnic Conflict and International Politics in the Middle East*. (Gainesville: The University Press of Florida, 1999).

Abbas Milani, *Eminent Persians*. Vol. 1, (Syracuse: Syracuse University Press, 2008).

Shaul Mishal and Avraham Sela, *The Palestinian Hamas: Vision, Violence and Coexistence*. (NY: Columbia University Press, 2000).

Assaf Moghadam, *The Globalization of Martyrdom*. (Baltimore: Johns Hopkins University Press, 2008).

Baqer Moin, *Khomeini: Life of the Ayatollah*. (London: I.B. Tauris, 2009).

Stephen R. Ward, *Immortal A Military History of Iran and Its Armed Forces*. (Washington, D.C.: Georgetown University Press, 2009).

Lawrence C. Wright, *The Looming Tower Al-Qaida and the Road to 9/11*. (NY: Alfred Knopf, 2006).

# ARTICLES

Ali Alfoneh, "How Intertwined Are the Revolutionary Guards in Iran's Economy?" *AEI Middle Eastern Outlook*, October 22, 2007, www.irantracker.org/analysis/how-intertwined-are-revolutionary-guards-irans-economy.

Greg Bruno, *Iran's Revolutionary Guards*, Council of Foreign Relations' Backgrounder, June 22, 2009, www.cfr.org/iran/irans-revolutionary-guards/p14324.

Anthony H. Cordesman with Adam C. Seitz, *Iranian Weapons of Mass Destruction: Biological Weapons Program*, CSIS, Draft Report, October 28, 2008, http://csis.org/files/media/csis/pubs/081028_iranbw_chapterrev.pdf.

Anthony H. Cordesman, *Iran's Revolutionary Guards, the Al-Quds Force, and Other Intelligence and Paramilitary Forces*, CSIS, August 16, 2007, http://csis.org/files/media/csis/pubs/070816_cordesman_report.pdf.

Anthony H. Cordesman, *Iran's Support of the Hezbollah in Lebanon*, CSIS, July 15, 2006 http://csis.org/files/media/csis/pubs/060715_hezbollah.pdf.

Matthew M. Frick, "Iran's Islamic Revolutionary Guard Corps: An Open Source Analysis," *Joint Force Quarterly*, Issue 49, 2nd Quarter, 2008, www.dtic.mil/cgi-bin/GetTRDoc?Location=U2&doc=GetTRDoc.pdf&AD=ADA516529.

Reuel Marc Gerecht, "Going Rogue —Hossein Ali Montazeri, 1922-2009," *The Weekly Standard*, January 4, 2010, Vol. 15, No. 16, www.weeklystandard.com/Content/Public/Articles/000/000/017/390wrflv.asp.

Jerry Guo, "Letter from Tehran: Iran's New Hardliners," *Foreign Affairs*, September 30, 2009, www.foreignaffairs.com/features/letters-from/letter-from-tehran-irans-new-hard-liners.

Elliot Hen-Tov and Nathan Gonzalez, "The Militarization of Post-Khomeini Iran: Praetorianism 2.0," *The Washington Quarterly*, Vol. 34, No. 1, Winter 2011, pp. 45-59.

Kenneth Katzman, *Iran-Iraq Relations,* CRS Report for Congress, August 13, 2010, www.fas.org/sgp/crs/mideast/RS22323.pdf.

Mehdi Khalaji, "Iran's Revolutionary Guard Corps, Inc.," *Policy Watch 1273*, The Washington Institute for Near East Policy, August 12, 2007, www.washingtoninstitute.org/templateC05.php?CID=2649.

Mehdi Khalaji, "Militarization of the Iranian Judiciary," *Policy Watch 1567*, Washington Institute for Near East Policy, August 13, 2009 http://washingtoninstitute.org/templateC05.php?CID=3105.

Fareed Mohamedi & Raad Alkadiri, "Iran: U.S. Sanctions, Iranian Responses and Implications for

Investment," A Special Presentation for Petrofed, June 14, 2010, http://petrofed.winwinhosting. net/upload/14june10/summary.pdf.

*Murder at Mykonos: The Anatomy of a Political Assassination*, Iran Human Rights Documentation Center, 2007, www.iranomid.com/en/ARCHVS/murder_at_mykonos_report.pdf.

Bruce Riedel, "The Clinton Administration," *Iran Primer*, United States Institute of Peace, http:// iranprimer.usip.org/resource/clinton-administration.

Steve Schippert, "Holes and Questions in the IAEA Iran Report," *ThreatsWatch.org*, February 27, 2008, http://threatswatch.org/analysis/2008/02/iaea-schweizer-kase/.

Shimon Shapira, "The Fantasy of Hezbollah Moderation," *Jerusalem Issue Brief*, Vol. 10, No. 2, May 23, 2010, www.jcpa.org/JCPA/Templates/ShowPage.asp?DBID=1&LNGID=1&TMID=11 1&FID=283&PID=0&IID=3983.

Ali Shariati, "Jihad and Shahadat. A Discussion of Shahid," www.shariati.com/english/jihadand.html.

Ali Shariati, "Red Shi'ism: The Religion of Martyrdom, Black Shi'ism: the Religion of Mourning," www.shariati.com/english/redblack.html.

Roozbeh Shafshekhan & Farzan Sabet, "The Ayatollah's Praetorians: The Islamic Revolutionary Guard Corps and the 2009 Election Crisis," *The Middle East Journal* Vol. 64, No. 4, Autumn 2010.

Allan Urry, "Why did Iran register ships in the Isle of Man?" BBC File on 4, July 14, 2010, www. bbc.co.uk/news/10604897.

Frederic Wherley et al., *The Rise of the Pasdaran*, RAND Corporation, 2009.

# D O C U M E N T S

Richard Armitage, *America's Challenges in a Changed World*, remarks at the United States Institute of Peace Conference, September 5, 2002, http://web.archive.org/web/20020917202341/ www.state.gov/s/d/rm/2002/13308pf.htm.

Bank Sepah's Annual Report for 2008-2009, www.banksepah.ir/DesktopModules/Contents/ assets/documents/Reports/2008-2009_Annual_Report.pdf

Complete List of Companies Controlled by the Foundation of the Oppressed, www.irmf.ir/en/ EN-RelatedCompanies.aspx

DIOMIL Company Website: www.diomil.ir/en/aboutus.aspx

English Translation of Iran's Constitution: www.iranonline.com/iran/iran-info/government/ constitution.html

Iran Watch Entity Listing, www.iranwatch.org/suspect/records/Kala-Naft.html

Iranian National Petrochemical Company Profile, www.iranwatch.org/suspect/records/national-petrochemical-company.html

"IRGC's Dominance over Iran's Politics and Economy: Part 1," *Iran Focus*, May 11, 2010, www.iranfocus.com/en/index.php?option=com_content&view=article&id=20355:irgcs-dominance-over-irans-politics-and-economy--part-1&catid=32:exclusive-reports&Itemid=32

Japanese Red Army (JRA), Anti-Imperialist International Brigade (AIIB), *Federation of American Scientists*, www.fas.org/irp/world/para/jra.htm

Letter from the Revolutionary Guards Commanders, 19 July 1999, www.iranian.com/News/1999/July/irgc.html

List of Murdered Iranian Dissidents from Various Political and Ethnic Backgrounds, www.iran-e-azad.org/english/terrorlist.html

OFAC's Specially Designated Nationals List, www.treasury.gov/ofac/downloads/t11sdn.pdf

PCC UK Company Details, www.companiesintheuk.co.uk/ltd/petrochemical-commercial-company-%28uk%29

Rahyab Rayaneh Gostar Company History, www.tidewater.ir/English/Companys/En_Rahyab.aspx

Reserve Bank of Australia's Iran Annex, *Attachment A to Sanctions Against Iran, Amendment to the Annex*, www.rba.gov.au/media-releases/2010/mr-10-18-attach-a.html

Sepasad Engineering Co.'s List of Projects, www.sepasad.com/en/index.php?option=com_phoc agallery&view=categories&Itemid=50

Text of Executive Order 13553, September 28, 2010, www.treasury.gov/resource-center/sanctions/Documents/13553.pdf

Tidewater Middle East Co. PLC Website, www.tidewater.ir/English/EN_Home.aspx
"Treasury Designates Multi-Million Dollar Procurement Network for Directly Supporting Iran's Missile Program," United States Department of Treasury Press Release, February 1, 2011, http://www.treasury.gov/press-center/press-releases/Pages/tg1044.aspx

United Nations Office on Drug and Crime, *World Drug Report 2010*, www.unodc.org/documents/wdr/WDR_2010/World_Drug_Report_2010_lo-res.pdf
United Nations Security Council Resolution 1747, www.iaea.org/newscenter/focus/iaeairan/unsc_res1747-2007.pdf.

U.S. Department of Defense, *Unclassified Report on Military Power in Iran*, April 2010, www.iranwatch.org/government/us-dod-reportmiliarypoweriran-0410.pdf

United States Bureau of Industry and Security Records, www.bis.doc.gov/news/2009/tdo_01232009.pdf

United States Department of the Treasury Office of Foreign Assets Control List of Specially Designated Nationals and Blocked Persons, July 29, 2011, www.treasury.gov/ofac/downloads/t11sdn.pdf

White House Executive Order on Iran's Human Rights' Abusers, September 29, 2010, www.america.gov/st/texttrans-english/2010/September/20100929190334su0.9839398.html, www.treasury.gov/resource-center/sanctions/Documents/13553.pdf, http://eurlex.europa.eu/LexUriServ/LexUriServ.do?uri=OJ:L:2011:100:0001:0011:EN:PDF

WikileaksCablegate, cable dated September 24, 2008, published in *Aftenposten*, www.aftenposten.no/spesial/wikileaksdokumenter/article3999428.ece

WikileaksCablegate, cable from the U.S. Embassy in Baku, March 6, 2009, http://cablesearch.org/cable/view.php?id=09BAKU175&hl=Singapore

# PRESS SOURCES

Ali Alfoneh, "The War over the War," *BBC Persian*, September 30, 2010, www.aei.org/article/102603.

Julian Borger & Robert Tait, "The Financial Power of the Revolutionary Guards," *The Guardian*, February 15, 2010, www.guardian.co.uk/world/2010/feb/15/financial-power-revolutionary-guard.

Massimo Calabresi, "New Iran Sanctions Target Iran Revolutionary Guards," *Time Magazine*, June 10, 2010, www.time.com/time/world/article/0,8599,1995603,00.html.

Marco Corti, "Produco Superbarche, Non Armi per Gli Ayatollah," Interview with Fabio Buzzi, *La Provincia di Lecco*, October 19, 2007.

Christopher De Bellaigue, "Cleric's Campaign Has Been Dogged by Murder Claims," *The Independent*, June 1, 2001, www.independent.co.uk/news/world/middle-east/clerics-campaign-has-been-dogged-by-murder-claims-686640.html.

Babak Dehghanpisheh, "Smugglers for the State," *Newsweek*, July 10, 2010, www.newsweek.com/2010/07/10/smugglers-for-the-state.html.

Christopher Dickey, R.M. Schneiderman & Babak Dehghanpisheh, "Shadow War," *Newsweek*, December 13, 2010, www.newsweek.com/2010/12/13/the-covert-war-against-iran-s-nuclear-program.html.

Guy Dinmore, "UK Speedboat Floats into Iran's Arms," *The Financial Times*, April 4, 2010, www.ft.com/cms/s/0/2be3b9c2-4021-11df-8d23-00144feabdc0.html#axzz1EDtMib4k.

Thomas Erdbrink, "Rallies close out Iranian campaign," *The Washington Post*, June 11, 2009, www.washingtonpost.com/wp-dyn/content/article/2009/06/10/AR2009061003548_pf.html.

Admiral Ali Fadavi's, *Mehr News*, February 7, 2011, www.mehrnews.com/en/newsdetail.aspx?NewsID=1248315.

Thomas Harding, "Iraqi Insurgents Using Austrian Rifles from Iran," *The Daily Telegraph*, February 13, 2007. www.telegraph.co.uk/news/worldnews/1542562/Iraqi-insurgents-using-Austrian-rifles-from-Iran.html

John Lancaster, "Khatemi, Iran's Ayatollah Gorbachev," *The Washington Post*, May 25, 1997.

Alexander U. Mathé, "Dochkeine Austro-WaffenimIrak," *Die Wiener Zeitung*, March 30, 2007, www.steyrarms.com/news/items/article/us-forces-contradict-newspaper-report-no-austrian-weapons-found-with-terrorists/?tx_ttnews[backPid]=9&cHash=87ced18815.

Stefania Maurizi & Gianluca Di Feo, "Cosí l'Italia Arma Teheran", *L'Espresso*, October 25, 2007, www.stefaniamaurizi.it/Inchieste/cosi_l_italia_arma_teheran.html.

Gcina Ntsaluba & Stefaans Brümmer, "How SA company Oiled Iran's War Machine," *Mail & Guardian Online*, September 24, 2010, www.mg.co.za/article/2010-09-24-how-sa-company-oiled-irans-war-machine.

Robin Pomeroy & Ramin Mostafavi, "Iran parliament makes military man oil minister," *Reuters*, August 3, 2011, www.reuters.com/article/2011/08/03/us-iran-oil-minister-vote-idUSTRE77220P20110803.

Claudia Rosett, "Iran's Hong Kong Shipping Shell Game," *The Wall Street Journal*, August 30, 2011, http://online.wsj.com/article/SB10001424053111904199404576536892392729816.html.

Tom Shanker, "Iran Encounter Grimly Echoes '02 War Game," *The New York Times*, January 12, 2008, www.nytimes.com/2008/01/12/washington/12navy.html.

Philip Sherwell, "Iran's 'Nuclear' University Conceals Research," *The Daily Telegraph*, April 16, 2006, www.telegraph.co.uk/news/worldnews/middleeast/iran/1515907/Irans-nuclear-university-conceals-research.html.

Amir Taheri, "Sudan: An expanding civil war with an Iran connection," *The New York Times*, April 9, 1997, www.nytimes.com/1997/04/09/opinion/09iht-edamir.t.html.

John J. Tkacik Jr., "The Arsenal of the Iraq Insurgency," *The Weekly Standard*, August 13, 2007, Vol. 12, No. 45, www.weeklystandard.com/Content/Public/Articles/000/000/013/956wspet.asp.

Mohammed Reza Yazdanpanah, "Former and Current Revolutionary Guard Commanders

Clash," *Rooz Online*, July 22, 2010, www.roozonline.com/english/news3/newsitem/article/former-and-current-revolutionary-guards-commanders-clash.html.

"Austria: Steyr-Mannlicher Arms Sales to Iran 'Legal'," *Turkish Weekly*, December 29, 2005, www.turkishweekly.net/news/24332/austria-steyr-mannlicher-arms-sale-to-iran-legal-.html.

"Iran's President names Revolutionary Guards Commander as Oil Chief" *Iran Focus*, November 16, 2005, www.iranfocus.com/en/index.php?option=com_content&view=article&id=4446:irans-president-names-revolutionary-guards-commander-as-oil-chief&catid=3:special-wire.

"Iran names Attacked Scientist Nuclear Chief: Report," *Reuters*, February 13, 2011, www.reuters.com/article/2011/02/13/us-iran-nuclear-chief-idUSTRE71C16F20110213.

"IRGC's Dominance Over Iran's Politics and Economy – Part 1," *Iran Focus*, May 11, 2010. www.iranfocus.com/en/index.php?option=com_content&view=article&id=20355:irgcs-dominance-over-irans-politics-and-economy--part-1&catid=32:exclusive-reports&Itemid=32.

"Miles Tops Charts in Rock and Roll Band," *The Daily Mail*, May 26, 2007, www.dailymail.co.uk/sport/othersports/article-457785/Miles-tops-charts-rock-roll-band.html.

"A New Alliance for Terror?" *Newsweek*, February 24, 1992, www.newsweek.com/1992/02/23/a-new-alliance-for-terror.html#.

"Revolutionary Guard buys stake in Iran Telecom," *New York Times Book Blog*, September 28, 2009, http://dealbook.nytimes.com/2009/09/28/revolutionary-guard-buys-stake-in-iran-telecom/

"Torpedo Launcher Boats Join IRGC Fleet," *Islami Davet*, August 10, 2010, www.islamidavet.com/english/2010/08/10/torpedo-launcher-boats-join-irgc-fleet/.

Emanuele Ottolenghi is a Senior Fellow at the Foundation for Defense of Democracies. He was born in Bologna, Italy. He completed his undergraduate studies at the University of Bologna and received his Ph.D. at the Hebrew University of Jerusalem. A senior consultant on Middle East Affairs, Dr. Ottolenghi has advised several foreign ministries and has testified before the Canadian and European parliaments on issues related to Iran. His extensive research exposed the connections between Iran's energy companies and its Islamic Revolutionary Guard Corps. He is a frequent commentator on Middle East affairs and transatlantic relations for many English-language and European-language publications such as *Il Sole 24 Ore,* Italy's financial daily, and his columns have appeared in many English- language publications, including *Commentary Magazine, National Review Online, Middle East Quarterly, The Guardian, The Australian, The Daily Mirror, The Daily Star,* and *The Wall Street Journal Europe.* He is the author, most recently, of *Iran: The Looming Crisis: Can the West live with Iran's nuclear threat?* (Profile Books, 2010).

Made in the USA
Charleston, SC
13 September 2011